A Teenag

Ron Tucker

A
Teenager's War

by
Ron Tucker

The World War II story of a young
Parachute Soldier

Foreword
by
Lt.-Gen. Sir Napier Crookenden

SPELLMOUNT
Staplehurst

British Library Cataloguing in Publication Data:
A catalogue record for this book is available
from the British Library

Copyright © Ron Tucker 1994

ISBN 1-873376-27-8

First published in the UK in 1994 by
Spellmount Limited
The Old Rectory
Staplehurst
Kent TN12 0AZ

Typeset by SX Composing, Rayleigh, Essex

Printed and bound by Antony Rowe Ltd, Eastbourne

To my grandchildren:

Newton, Natalie and Vanessa,

Lucyann, Richard and Kate

Contents

Foreword

by Lieutenant-General
Sir Napier Crookenden KCB DSO OBE DL

In the evening of July 26th 1944 I was sitting in the command post dug-out of Headquarters 6th Airlanding Brigade just West of the Bois de Bavent ridge in Normandy. As the brigade major, I was trying to work out the next day's patrol programme for our three glider-borne battalions, when the field telephone from Divisional Headquarters rang. It was the Chief of Staff, Lieutenant Colonel Bobby Bray. "You are to take over command of the 9th Parachute Battalion at once. Go up there tomorrow morning. They are down to 150 men, are very tired and you will have quite a job to do."

This was a marvellous opportunity for me, although I felt a little nervous at the prospect of command of a battalion of the Parachute Regiment. Although I had done my jumps, I was a major in the Cheshire Regiment and I wondered about my reception in this battalion of another regiment, cut down by death and wounds to so small a number.

I need not have worried. From the moment next day when I walked into their group of slit trenches amongst the fields, orchards and woods of that ridge, I was made welcome by every one of them, whatever his rank. My service with them for the rest of the War in Europe and for another 18 months in Palestine was the happiest and most rewarding time of my Army life. Ron Tucker's book explains why this was so, since so many of the Battalion shared with Ron Tucker the same cheerful, willing and vigorous outlook on life.

Through Normandy, Belgium, Holland and Germany Ron Tucker takes us with him into battle and out of it, into camps and billets, in English, Scots, French and Belgian civilian homes, into hospitals, and finally back to Middlesbrough and a happy life with his Dorothy. Now in 1994 nearly 200 of the Battalion still meet for our annual dinner and we keep up those friendships made 50 years ago. This book will give pleasure, not only to us, his old friends, but to everybody interested in those far-off days and in the nature of a young Englishman at war.

Napier Crookenden.

A NOTE ON THE BRITISH AIRBORNE FORCES

On 22nd June 1940 Mr Winston Churchill called for "the formation of a corps of at least five thousand parachute troops". Thus the foundation stone of Airborne Forces and The Parachute Regiment was laid. A Parachute Training School was quickly formed at Ringway, and No. 2 Commando (Army), later renamed No. 11 Special Air Service Battalion, became the first unit to be trained. By the end of 1940 over 500 officers and men had qualified for their coveted parachute wings.

In February 1941 the first British Airborne blow was struck with the destruction of the Tragino Aqueduct in Italy. This was followed in February 1942 by the capture and removal of a secret radar installation at Bruneval in German-occupied France.

From then onwards the operations of Airborne Forces increased in scope as the techniques were developed and more resources became available. In North Africa, the 1st Parachute Brigade was dropped on widely separated objectives, and in the subsequent fighting earned the name of 'The Red Devils'. This title was begrudgingly bestowed upon the regiment by the enemy in recognition of the now famous Red Beret.

In the attack on Sicily the same Brigade was dropped by night, with the task of seizing the Primosole Bridge. The 1st, 2nd and 4th Parachute Brigades then saw service in Italy. When the 1st and 4th Brigades returned to England before the invasion of Northern France, the 2nd Independent Parachute Brigade remained, then later took part in Airborne operations in Italy, Southern France and Greece.

The night of 5th/6th June 1944 marked the first Allied divisional Airborne Operations, with 6th Airborne Division landing in Normandy with the tasks of securing the left flank of the British seaborne assault on D-Day. The operation at Arnhem, which was part of Montgomery's plan to shorten the war by driving a wedge into the German front, followed on 17th September 1944. 2 Para held the bridge at Arnhem for 4 days but the armoured thrust was unable to link up. On 24th March 1945 the 6th Airborne Division were the first British troops to cross the River Rhine into Germany.

Chapter One

With the Gordons in Aberdeen

I am always lucky. I could easily have landed a hundred yards away into deep swamps and sunk straight to the bottom with eighty pounds of equipment to pull me down. One hundred and ninety-two of my friends did: almost one third of the 9th Parachute Battalion wiped out in a few minutes.

It was dark, but I could see a small road winding its way between water-filled fields, and I was coming down for a dry landing on the grass. My rifle was packed in a felt sleeve on the end of a nylon rope, which was caught up in the hedge between the road and the field. Before I could get to it to protect myself, three of the thousands of Panzer and SS troops and Hitler Youth we were told would be waiting for us, rushed up the road toward me. I was armed to the teeth with machine-gun magazines, an anti-tank mine, a smoke grenade, two '36' Mills hand grenades, four sticks of plastic explosive, and fifty rounds of '303' ammo for rifle and Bren gun, but my rifle had to be unpacked before I could use it. I jumped over the hedge and, lying parallel to it, pulled the pin from one of the grenades.

The adrenalin was flowing, and I held my breath, listening to the soldiers who had arrived on the scene talking as they examined my 'chute. I could tell that the fourth soldier, who came riding up on a bicycle, was an NCO. He gave some order, I suppose, to look for me, because they came to the hedge and peered into the darkness across the water in the field. One of them had his jack-boot so close to my nose, I could smell the oily leather. It can only have been two or three minutes before they all ran off as quickly as they came, but it seemed like hours to me.

We had been instructed not to start private battles on our own, but to make for the Battalion meeting point, called the RV or rendez-vous, so I resisted the temptation to throw the grenade after them. We had an important gun battery to destroy before daylight, otherwise the landing-craft reaching Sword Beach next morning would be blown to pieces in the water. It was D-Day 1944, time 0045 hours.

*

Although my dear father had no idea that in just under two years his son would be one of the first Allied soldiers to land in Normandy, he must have had some idea that I could be in danger sooner or later, even when I had been a Gordon Highlander. He had taken time off work to see me off at Middlesbrough station at 8am on the 6th August 1942, which was my first day as a soldier. I was sixteen, not eighteen as it said on my travelling instructions.

For the previous six months I had been a member of the local defence volunteers, later called the Home Guard. I had fired a rifle on Guisborough Ranges, and fired a Northover projector, and learned very basic drills. Each week, I spent a night on guard duty at the power station in Snowdon Road. One night during an air raid, at a time when we expected to be invaded from the skies by the German Para, the old soldier who used to share duty with me, and who was over seventy, said to me, 'My eyes are not as good as yours, but if you see a German parachutist just point my rifle at him and I'll pull the trigger.'

I realise now how worried my parents must have been when I left home to enlist, and I admire their decision to allow me to go away into the Army at such a critical period of the War years. One word from them about my age could have put an end to my service. They had so much more courage than I. Apart from the odd week camping with the Cubs and Scouts, I had never been away from home, with its comforts and good food. Even in the 1930s, my father had a good job and we did not go short of anything.

Everyone said, 'The army food is terrible, the barracks are uncomfortable, and in two weeks you will want to come back home.' All this had little effect on me, but when the Recruiting Officer said to me that, as a volunteer, I could have a choice of regiments, I decided to get as far away from home as possible, so that it would be very difficult to get home even if the stories were true! A map on the wall was dotted with small flags showing each regimental training camp in England and Scotland. A flag at Aberdeen was as far up north as any, and I enquired about this one.

'That's the Gordon Highlanders, lad; is that where you want to go?'

'It will do fine, Sergeant, so get me up there as soon as possible.'

By lunch time on my first day, the train was passing over the Forth Bridge. 'Aberdeen is still four hours off, son; don't worry, we don't go any further, so you won't miss the stop', the ticket collector assured me. At five o'clock we pulled into Aberdeen Station at last, and I stepped out into Scotland for the first time. I must have looked like a recruit, because a soldier said 'You for the Gordons? Follow me.' I joined twenty other lads in a bus painted dark green, and in no time we sped off through the town toward Brig o' Don Barracks.

There was little time to get to know anyone at the barracks, there was so much to do: have a meal, draw bedding from the stores and provide a lot of information to the orderly for documentation. I just got my bed made before lights out in the hut at 11pm. The bed was a bit rough: there were no sheets, not even a pillow, and no pyjamas to wear between the four coarse blankets, but I slept well.

A very strange noise outside the hut next morning made me nearly jump out of my skin. It sounded like an animal choking. I had never heard bagpipes before. Two pipers commenced their duty by playing reveille and marching up and down the line of timber huts, followed by the Orderly Corporal shouting at anyone still in bed when he opened the door. I had not yet started to shave, so the cold-water wash did not bother me. The Company Sergeant Major inspected us first thing and asked me if I had shaved.

'No, sir', I replied.

'Why not?'

I told him that I had not started to shave yet, and he told me, 'From now on you will go through the motions, just to get used to it', and I did.

After breakfast we met our Platoon Sergeant, called Kirk, from Glasgow. He was in the Highland Light Infantry, and his Corporal was a Gordon. Between them it was their job to turn thirty civvies into a disciplined platoon, in dress and in bearing. We marched and drilled for hours, until our new boots started to bend more easily. The inoculations and vaccinations were carried out on a Friday afternoon, which put most of us out of action till Monday morning.

We attended quite a few lectures on various subjects, from current affairs to military law, history and religion. The Medical Officer told us about diseases and infections, also the painful treatment required if pox or gonorrhoea was contracted. These educated lecturers used a new language strange to my ears, and a vocabulary of words I had never heard before. I discovered a new thing called an Oxford accent, not found in my part of the world. Education took on a new meaning. From leaving school at the age of thirteen, when the war started, and commencing work in an office in the steel works at Dorman and Long's Britannia Works, the only thing I had heard was every kind of foul language possible. I regretted not having taken my schooling more seriously.

On the fourth day, during a drill period on the square, my name was called and I was told to report to the dental hut. I joined a small queue. There were two dentists working very fast indeed, and in no time I was seated in the chair and a Colonel in the Army Dental Corps was holding my head with his left hand while he drilled five fillings. They were only small patches of decay in each tooth, but the size of the holes drilled and filled was enormous. The work only took ten minutes to complete, but no pain-killer was administered. I had never experienced anything like it before, and it was so unpleasant that my bottom hardly touched the seat for more than a second at a time. Reporting back to the Sergeant on the square, I found the drill continuing as if nothing had happened, though I was still shaking. But those fillings have lasted, and are still intact after 46 years.

The recruits were a mixed bag. The oldest one was in his early forties, and arrived in camp wearing a ten-gallon hat, having paid his own fare from South America. He was well over six feet tall, with enormous hands; his parents had come from Scotland. There was a local lad who had come from a farm just outside Aberdeen; he had great difficulty in co-ordinating his arms to swing when marching, and he kept on going when the Sergeant told him to halt. His left arm came up at the same time as he stepped out with his left foot, and the Sergeant used to call out, 'Whoa! You are not ploughing now, Private Wood.'

Basil Whitley came from Hull, and could play an accordion very well. There were three lads from the West Riding of Yorkshire, and five from London who had all attended private schools and had learned to shoot during their Cadet training. There was a very nice chap from Edinburgh, and one from Glasgow recently released from detention. Birmingham was represented by Bill Leggett. Private Mc Gregor came from Oxford; his father had served with the Gordons during the First World War. We were all very keen to learn.

16

One of the recruits was an ex-policeman from Liverpool. He had a very high opinion of himself and few people liked him. He provoked me by stepping into a shower cubicle I had prepared one afternoon, but I accepted discipline and managed to keep out of trouble. The next day we had just completed a session in the gym, there was time to spare, and the Sergeant gave me two pairs of boxing gloves, saying, 'Get yourself a partner.' I passed the other pair of gloves to the policeman from Liverpool and we got into the ring. He was late into the dining hall for dinner, but when he did arrive, after a visit to the medical centre, there was a roar of laughter which brought him down to size, as he could not conceal his black eye.

My circle of friends increased overnight, but I found that Sergeant Kirk had placed my name in the boxing team for 'B' Company.

I had been brought up to hand over my pay to my mother, who would give me part of it back for pocket money, so it was natural that half my 21 shillings (£1.05p) weekly pay should be allotted for sending home. Soap, toothpaste, polish and blanco had to be bought, and my 10 shillings soon disappeared. Quite a few members of the platoon who came from private schools had extra money sent from home. Ways of supplementing my pay had to be found. Each Saturday morning the whole training centre was on parade in shorts before setting out on a cross-country run of some five miles, and the first five returning were given savings stamps by the CO. I came to rely on the 5 shillings which I usually won. The winner received 30 shillings, but I never managed to be the first back.

The first granite building through the barrack gates was a guard room the size of a bungalow; outside stood a tall flag pole flying the Union Jack, with a neat, square base of white painted stones. The garden around the guard room was very tidy and even the flowers seemed to be stood to attention. The door handle, letter box and fire buckets outside were all very highly polished. On entering, the smell of polish was overpowering, and the parquet floor reflected everything like a mirror. In front of a table a yard-square grill on the floor had a mirror beneath it, a relic from peace-time soldiering, so that inspection under the kilt could be made while a soldier was stood to attention.

Seated at the table was a regimental police corporal over six feet tall, with broad shoulders and a voice like thunder. A red door behind him shut the cells off from the main room. Anyone unfortunate enough to be held in the cells had a terrible life, and was the energy behind all the polishing. It was said among the lads that the Police Corporal could place a man in the cells for the slightest misbehaviour.

After our first week's training, we could leave the barracks and visit the town of Aberdeen, but first our dress had to meet with the Police Corporal's approval: should a button be undone, or dirt be seen beneath the nails, should there be unpolished brasses on belt or cap badge, or not enough polish on our boots as we stood to attention on the grill, while he counted the number of studs, then the fault had to be corrected in the barrack room. This meant walking back around the square, putting the matter right, and joining the queue again. It could take over an hour, if you were not passed the first time. The faint-hearted just gave up and spent the evening in the NAAFI.

On returning from town the procedure was the same: march in, stand to attention on the grill reporting name and number, while a policeman placed a tick against your name in the book. Anyone not able to stand perfectly still was considered to be under the influence of drink and placed in a cell.

By the time we had reached the fourth week's training, a loose bar in the railings was discovered at the back of the barracks. A privileged few knew about this, and it made life much easier for both leaving and returning.

In town a YMCA ran a good canteen staffed by volunteer women, usually older women, very kind-hearted, who were taken advantage of whenever I was short of money, which was pretty often. It was easy just to order several things, like bacon and eggs, beans, and tomatoes and, before they were on the plate, to ask how much it would cost, holding a few coins in the hand and counting them. It always worked: 'Are you short of money, son?', and they waived payment, even giving extra cakes and tea, all free. They really were lovely people.

On Sunday evenings, each church in Union Street, and there were quite a few, had representatives asking you to attend a short service. After a few hymns and prayers, curtains would be drawn back, revealing large tables full of plates of cakes and sandwiches, large teapots and mugs. In one evening you could visit up to three churches, and really feel as though you could eat no more. Perhaps it was just as well that it only occurred once a week! It meant we could afford to go to the pictures two or three nights during the week.

The boxing team had quite a few privileges: while the rest of the Company were doing route marches or cleaning up the

18

barracks, we would be exercising in the gym or sparring in the ring, or swimming in the sea just at the back across the golf links. It was great fun and I enjoyed keeping fit. I was sure I could feel myself growing with all the exercise and fresh air.

One evening in Aberdeen, we sat at the end of King Street watching an old piper playing outside a pub. He had a box on the floor to collect coppers from passers-by, and each time he passed the box as he walked up and down he would make a quick calculation. As soon as he had enough for a pint, he would tuck his pipes under his arm and make a quick entry into the pub. Later on when we saw him again the tune was not as good, but he could still play, though he could hardly walk in a straight line. He was well known in the area, and played every night for his enjoyment and beer money.

Only a few weeks had passed since I had left home, but I had been exposed to all kinds of vice. I managed to keep on the right track. I tried to stay clear of drinking beer, but one night when I was in the company of two lads we visited a pub in Union Street. By the time we reached the counter the drinks had been pulled: the barman said it had been taken care of. Aberdonians are anything but mean; I found them to be very generous people indeed. The beer tasted awful, and I did not bother with it again for years.

The market in the centre of Union Street was covered in and had a first floor. The stalls had very little on them in 1942, apart from a few antiques and old clothes. Every stall had young girls hanging around the back, near rooms with net curtains at the windows. One Saturday afternoon we realised we were in the middle of a brothel, though the girls had not approached us, as it was well known that recruits had very little money. They were looking out for seamen from the boats in the harbour at the bottom of the street.

Pay was handed out after barrack room inspection on Saturday mornings, and this was followed by a cross-country run. After dinner we could leave camp for the rest of the day if we wished. The Corporal in charge of the platoon hut, a Gordon with some service experience (he must have been about thirty-five, and an old man as far as I was concerned), asked me if I would like to play cards, he would show me how. I had not played cards in my life before, and I got worried when I saw all the money on the table, so I declined; however, he persuaded six other lads to join him, and when I returned at tea-time from town he had won most of the money from the boys. Before lights out, he had cleaned them out completely. It was a good lesson learned at their expense, the result being that I am still unable to play cards to this day. Sad to say, the same lads were there again next Saturday and once more lost all their pay.

Sunday morning was church parade. We would wear our best battle dress, and the whole training centre would parade, with the band in full dress with their kilts swinging, and off we would march along King Street to Aberdeen. I thoroughly enjoyed it, and loved to hear the band play.

I was very shy when it came to girls and never found anyone to go out with, but I enjoyed learning to dance, though I must have given my partners some very sore feet with my size nines. One of my friends was put on duty without warning, and asked me to do him a favour by delivering a message to his girl friend. I went off to a residential area of Aberdeen, which had some very fine detached granite houses. The long paths leading up to the granite stairways were very imposing. I began to wonder if he had given me the right address.

A bell on the end of a huge chain announced my presence at the large oak door with studs in it. A maid invited me into a hall with stained glass windows and oak-panelled stairway, and returned after a few minutes to say that someone would see me. A lady about as old as my mother came out of a room, and I could tell she was going to be difficult by the look on her face.

'I understand you want to see my daughter, young man.'

'Not exactly; you see, I have a message for her from her friend, who was unfortunately detained.'

'Why could he not write?'

'There was no time, as they were to meet tonight', I replied, and as soon as I had said that I realised it made things worse.

'My daughter does not see anyone without a formal introduction, and I have no knowledge of her being in the company of a member of the armed forces. Kindly tell your friend that she will not be allowed to see him again. Goodnight.'

I was glad to get out of the house, but was concerned for the girl, who was probably in for a bad time.

During training everyone had taken aptitude tests, and also written tests. I had found the mechanical and fitting tests easy, while the lads from the public schools found difficulties assembling gear wheels and ball bearings. On the other hand, they rattled away at the maths and written tests, while I struggled with the first page. My English was atrocious. Until leaving home I had not needed to write letters, but now it was the only way to communicate, since my home was not on the telephone. In an emergency I could ring the house next door, but it had to be important.

Our weapon training was improving. Most of us could group five rounds in a four-inch (10cm) circle at 100 yards with the rifle and Bren machine-gun. We also fired the Sten machine-gun automatic, and the revolver; we handled anti-tank mines and threw grenades on the ranges.

Towards the end of six weeks we marched to Cruden Bay, near Peterhead. Five miles of coastline had been cleared of civilians, and we used the empty farm houses to live in and cook our meals. During two days of field firing we had a marvellous time, shooting off hundreds of rounds of ammunition at anything in the area, including rabbits in the big sand hills. Piles of tins on the beach set up like a coconut shy would be riddled with holes after a machine-gun practice. We were told we must get used to the noise of guns firing at random.

It was time to think of our next move: to a battalion for further training. A Gordon battalion was stationed in the Shetlands, and it was said to be a dreadful posting during war time, with only the NAAFI to spend off-duty hours in. Two boys from public schools were sent to officer training units. My name was down for a driving course at the Linkfield School near the football field in Aberdeen.

Before then, the Company boxing match was to be held, and then the Battalion match. I won the Company match on points, and did not get hurt. The Battalion match was quite a big affair, with the gym packed full and people attending who had come from all over the area. The lad I was to fight was not quite as tall as I was, but just the same weight. He was 24 and quite experienced, and gave me a run for my money. In the third round he gave me a punch on the nose which made me see stars, and I was glad when the fight was over as I could not have gone on much longer. My eyes were closing up, my face was swollen and it was an effort to make my way back to the barrack room, where I just dropped on my bed almost out of breath. Next morning I had to report sick and was taken to Woodhead Hospital, where a specialist announced I had a broken nose. He said the swelling was stopping my breathing and would recede in a day or two. He was right: in three days I was able to breathe, through one nostril anyway!

The Battalion Match was the climax to our six weeks at Brig o' Don Barracks. A day later we all moved on to our next posting.

Chapter 2

A Volunteer for the Parachute Regiment

At Linkfield School the atmosphere was a little less demanding than at the Barracks, though an enthusiastic Corporal used to take the names of six lads in our room every morning, mainly, I think, because ours was one of the first ones he visited. He would open the door and shout 'Get up!', close it, then open it straight away. Since I was, naturally, not up, my name was taken every day for the first week. I had to report to the kitchens after the day's work, and clean up all the pans and cooking tins. Some were as big as a baby's bath. Six sacks of potatoes also had to be peeled for the next day.

The ATS Sergeant was not bad provided she was satisfied with your work, and would make a grand supper of eggs, fried bread, slab cake and tea with sugar in it. It passed the night away in a warm place, and saved having to buy food, as our last meal was at 5pm.

Our driving instructor would carry a dip stick two feet long in his hand and bring it down on the back of the hand if a mistake was made changing gear, or if the speed limit was exceeded. It was October; the weather was closing in after a lovely warm summer. It was cold driving along the esplanade in a fifteen-hundredweight truck with an open cab and just a canvas top. There were trams to avoid in the town, and cobble stones that were wet and slippery in bad weather, and the streets leading down to the harbour were steep and narrow. It was actually a first-class place to learn to drive, as none of the routes was straightforward.

Motor cycles and Bren gun carriers with tracks on were parked in the school yard after the day's training was over. With a guard at the entrance, another guard would patrol along the vehicles; seven men would report for guard mounting, and one would be excused duty for neat appearance. The officer inspecting and mounting the guard would decide who was the smartest on parade. On my first guard, I was lucky and became 'Stick Man', which meant that I could fall out once guard mounting was over. It was a laborious task pressing and pleating the uniform, blanco-ing equipment, cleaning rifle and bayonet till they were spotless, but nevertheless well worth it if the result was to be excused duty.

Some of the well-off public school boys were also at Linkfield, and one of them who was detailed for duty on guard asked me if I would do it for him, and offered me five shillings. Of course I said I would, if he cleaned my kit to wear, and an hour later, with five shillings in my pocket, I saw him at the tram stop, waiting to go into Aberdeen. I became quite experienced at the drill, and got Stick Man again and again.

Having been selected at one such guard mounting, I was over confident and almost messed my chances up. I expected the next word of command from the Orderly Officer to be 'Stick Man fall out'. I would have turned to the right and marched across the square to stand beside the Orderly Sergeant until the guard had marched off to their duties. The Officer said something and I at once turned right; then I realised he was telling someone else to stand still. I froze to the spot: I thought, 'This is it, I have had it!' My face must have been red. Perhaps word had got around that I had been doing someone else's guard mountings and they took pity on me, for nothing was said; I had pulled it off again.

I still got caught for cook-house duties every now and then, and on one of these duties a piece of the wire which was used to clean the pans got lodged in my finger. I did not notice it until one night when, as I left a cinema, my friend had to help me on with my overcoat, as my left arm would not bend. Next morning I could not get dressed, and the Corporal placed me on the sick list. We marched up the road to Sunnybank School, where the doctor held his surgery, and standing outside his room in line, waiting my turn, I must have passed out. When I came to, it was to see him lancing my finger, which was full of poison. He took me in his car to Brig o' Don Barracks, where one room was fitted out as a hospital ward. I had noticed it while stationed there, but had never had occasion to visit it.

The next three days passed very quickly, as I slept all the time, only waking to have hot lint poultices put on the red patch on my arm. The fourth day was my seventeenth birthday, and I woke to find three birthday cards from home. Recovery was remarkable once the poison had gone from my system, but by the time I had returned to my course I had lost ten days' driving training, and soon it would be time to sit the tests. Failure would mean doing it all again.

We were all taken up on the moors, to some rough country a few miles beyond Aberdeen. There were pot holes full of water and thick mud everywhere, just like on a battlefield. The CO explained what was going on and how to negotiate the course, and the Senior Instructor gave us a demonstration. He speeded up the engine just as it seemed he would never get out of the hole the vehicle was in, up to its axles in thick mud, and passing through water nearly a yard deep he used first gear to prevent it from stalling. On his return to the starting point, the CO said, 'Now that's how it's done; does anyone think he could take it through the course without stalling the engine?'

Like a shot, I dashed out, jumped into the truck and made off, before anyone could answer him. I thought, if I could do this I would be sure of making up for my lost time in hospital and get a pass the next week.

It was just luck, I suppose, that the wheels kept turning and the two-inch tread on the tyres pulled it through all the obstacles. Half-way round I heard my mates cheering me on, and when finally I arrived back at the starting point I felt great, and was sure the officers would remember when some points were given out and that I would pass the course. The CO just said, 'Well done, lad.'

The driving test lasted an hour, going up and down the steep streets of Aberdeen, parking on hills leading to the docks, and reversing into tight corners. We had been well taught, and every one of us passed the course.

By December we had been in the Army four months, which qualified us for a free railway ticket and seven days' leave. My parents were pleased to see me, and I was glad to be home again; it seemed a long time since I had left. I am sure that my mother had been saving up rations, so that she could give me a feed worth remembering. It was not until I tasted her food again that I realised that Army food could be rough at times. Most of my friends were working very hard in the steel works, although Fred Wright had joined the Navy and expected to be posted very soon. We usually met at a milk bar in Linthorpe Road, where we drank milk shakes by the dozen, at twopence-halfpenny each.

A week before Christmas I was posted to Sunnybank School, a holding unit, to wait for posting to a battalion as Driver I/C. Nothing special happened: there were a few drill periods during each day, and each morning before breakfast we ran and marched around the streets of Aberdeen in the dark for an hour. It kept us fit, and after breakfast there was always work to be done in the kitchens peeling sack after sack of potatoes. That was how I spent Christmas Day, peeling all day long. Scottish Regiments do not make any arrangements for Christmas.

When the list of names for duties came up on the notice board on New Year's Eve, they were all of English lads. Twelve of us paraded , and the Scottish Sergeant read our instructions out: no-one was allowed to leave the barracks, and if a fire started, we had to deal with it until the fire brigade arrived! 'On no account will you disobey these orders!' Then in a lower tone of voice, almost a whisper, he said, 'But I am not a Sassenach like you guys, so I will be leaving you to look after things till I come back.' On the first floor our barrack room windows looked over the gates, and as soon as we saw the Sergeant leave, we smartly followed on his heels.

Basil Whitley from Hull, Henry Ford from Bradford and I made our way down towards King Street to see what all the excitement was. We had heard that everyone went mad in Scotland at Hogmanay and it was certainly going to be an experience for all of us so-called Sassenachs. Turning down towards the town past a terrace of smart granite houses, we could hear laughter coming from the third house. As we reached the garden gate it was flung open and a crowd of young people came running out. We found ourselves pulled along in a chain of excited, happy people, and the leader took us round the side of the house, along a short passage leading to the back entrance.

We could hardly believe our eyes when the door closed after us; it was obvious that we had been captured as their guests for Hogmanay! The tables were laden with every kind of food: meat pies, cakes, fruit etc. They must have been saving up rations for months to produce such a grand display in wartime. The large table in the centre of the room was for use as an air-raid shelter, called a Morrison shelter after a minister in the Cabinet. There was a smaller table in the corner of the room loaded with bottles of spirit and a small barrel of beer. Canned beer was unheard of in 1942.

At seventeen years old, working hard from 6am till 5pm burned up a lot of energy, so I was forever hungry and never seemed to get enough to eat, but that night I finished up unable to find room for another crumb. We were singing and dancing most of the night, till we just dropped on the floor in heaps to sleep till daylight, when it all started again. It was good, clean fun, with all the family taking part. Grandma was sitting in front of the fire having a nice, quiet drink, or a 'wee dram' as the Scots people called it, and enjoying watching us all dance and enjoy ourselves.

In the five months since my arrival in Aberdeen, I had become very fond of the people there; wherever we went we could tell that they were pleased to see us, and everyone was most kind and helpful. I knew that very soon we would move down south, and I was not looking forward to parting with such good friends.

It was the night following New Year's Day, and visions of the 'glasshouse' loomed large in my mind. We had been absent without leave, a very serious offence in the Army. All three of us made our way back to the camp at 4.30am and moved quietly into our barrack room. We were fully dressed, but put a blanket over each of us. The next thing we knew, reveille sounded, the lights went on, we washed and had breakfast and not once were we asked where we had been. It seemed we had not been missed, and in fact I don't think anyone had been back very long! So we just carried on as if nothing had happened.

In the short time I was at Aberdeen I had learned a lot about human nature; knowing how to live in a room with twenty other people was an achievement in itself. The contrasts were truly amazing: on one side of me slept a public school boy and on the other a rough Glaswegian who had just come out of prison, but both were good friends of mine. Posting was to a young soldiers' battalion in Norfolk. I was sorry I was leaving Aberdeen, and wondered if I would ever see it again.

A party of twenty of us left on the 6pm train for Peterborough. It was the 10th January on our arrival at a wooded camp near Fakenham at 10am the following day. We were introduced to the most uncomfortable accommodation imaginable: mud and water on a well-trodden route through the camp, with thick snow in places untrodden. The dining room was a large tent with duck-boards on the floor to keep you from sinking into the mud.

The sleeping arrangments in the Nissen huts were unbelievable. There were double bunk beds so close together that it was difficult to move between them. Our hut had a very small stove in the centre of the room, with a chimney going straight through the roof. One bucket of coal per day burned away in less than two hours. Condensation ran down the corrugated walls in little streams, and it was so cold that, even with a great-coat on over the four blankets, I had to sleep with my socks on. We collected wood from nearby trees, but it was so wet that it was difficult to burn. The driver sleeping beneath me was from my home town of Middlesbrough. His name was Ron Sturdy and he was a Royal Scot trained at Carlisle. We became good friends, and it was nice to be able to talk about places at home familiar to us both.

Our job was to take young soldiers to farms and factories in the area, where they would work during the day, and we then brought them back at dusk. As drivers, we had to stay with the vehicles and did not see much of the work carried out, but most of it had to do with sugar beet, both in the fields and in the factories.

Before leaving the camp each morning, every man would collect his haversack rations for the midday meal, usually sandwiches of cheese or tinned fish, supposed to be salmon. The smell of it put me right off, until I was so hungry that I was glad to eat it. I have disliked salmon ever since. The tea was contained in large dixies which turned it dark brown, almost black. It looked like coffee, after it had been standing for hours. Life in general was pretty miserable in every way.

Returning to our camp one afternoon, we read Company orders for the next day and alongside our instructions was a notice asking for volunteers for the Parachute Regiment. I immediately put my name down, thinking Ron Sturdy would do the same, but he would not hear of it. He said it was 'bloody dangerous', or words to that effect. He said 'You don't live long in that mob.' I was sorry that he felt that way, as he was as fit as I was and very strong, and I could not understand him not wanting to join.

We were still taking the lads out to the farms each day, and three days later we both had to take a detachment of 30 to a place called Littleport, near Ely in Cambridgeshire. After duty, we had a small canteen in a church hut to sit in, where volunteer ladies made beans on toast or bacon and eggs with tea for a few pence. There was a wireless to listen to, and a room for writing letters or reading books. Our huts were still of the Nissen type, but had single beds. It was in an old builder's yard which was concreted, so was dry and much better than the previous camp.

There may have been a bus to Ely at some time, but not when we wanted one, so we walked the seven miles to see what it was like. It had a beautiful cathedral and just one cinema, and we went in to find that the film was Walt Disney's *Dumbo*, which hardly seemed worth the fourteen miles' round trip!

On Sundays we went to church. To be honest, it was to miss the fatigues dealt out to those who stayed behind. Ron Sturdy was very shy and retiring, so I was surprised when he began talking to the girl sitting next to us in church. When we came out he introduced himself to her parents, and I could hardly believe my eyes as he walked off down the road with them. From that moment I saw very little of him during our free time.

My Aunt Liz had died. Her death was the first which I had experienced in the family; it upset me and I thought a lot about her. I asked the Company Commander for some leave and I was given seven days, though strictly speaking I was not due any leave till the end of February.

On my return to camp, late on a Sunday night, I found the Nissen huts in darkness. The electicity was turned off, but I could feel the beds had no blankets or mattresses. The only thing to do was to call at the Policeman's house in the village, to find out if he knew where everyone had gone. My ticket was on his desk. 'You have to go to Southend,' he said, ' but there won't be a train until morning.' He took me to a Mrs. Robinson who lived in the next street and belonged to the Salvation Army.

I must say that the Robinsons could not have been kinder, I was made so very welcome and they provided a meal and a bed made from an extending chair in the kitchen. I was given a lovely breakfast next morning, and they insisted on carrying some of my kit to the station. They were still waving on the platform when I lost sight of them as the steam from the engine obscured my view. I changed at Peterborough, King's Cross and Liverpool Street, so I saw some of London for the first time.

Southend was a holiday resort in peace time, and boasted the longest pier in England. The billets were empty boarding houses, and Ron Sturdy had saved me a bed in his room. He was pleased to see me, and gave me a guided tour of the town. We found out where all the cinemas and the snack bars were; the pier was closed for the duration of the war. He was writing to the girl he had met every few days.

For the next two weeks we cleaned and serviced the transport, and just as I was thinking what a waste of time it all was, Ron came running up with the news that I had to go to a hall in town to see if I was medically fit for the Para. Ten of us reported to the visiting team from the Airborne forces in a large church hall. We were told to strip off to our underpants. My initial being T meant a long, cold wait, and before it was my turn I was frozen stiff. An orderly said, 'Give me a sample of your water in there', and left me. On a small table stood 30 small glasses. I started to pee and could not stop, so I filled all the glasses. It was not surprising that the Orderly was mad: 'Now I will have to wash all of those out before the next man comes in! Why didn't you use the bucket under the table?'

At one stage of the examination I was really worried, because the Doctor said my hearing was not all that it should be. He decide to syringe my ears, and out came lumps of wax as big as my little finger: no wonder I could not hear properly. We all passed the medical, including the Sergeant Major, who volunteered with us.

A week later it was time to say goodbye to Ron Sturdy, as we had to report to Hardwick Camp, near Chesterfield, which was the basic training area for all potential Airborne troops. Ron still had no regrets, and wished me luck. The Sergeant Major was in charge of the party, and we all travelled up to Sheffield and reported to the Regimental Transport Officer, who arranged transport to Hardwick Camp.

Chapter 3

Hardwick Camp and Ringway; My Age is Discovered

On arrival Sergeant-Major Strachan was waiting to greet us: 'You will move about this camp at the double at all times except when you leave the dining room after a meal to return to your billets, but at any other time, even in the dark, if you are found walking you will have me to answer to.' He went on to say what would happen to us. We learned that he had just come out of hospital after treatment for three bullets that had passed through his guts on the Bruneval raid, the first time the Para had been used in France. We treated him with respect.

The camp was on the side of a hill and, while it was easy running down the slopes, it was very tiring running up, especially after a hard day's training. We had been formed into sticks of ten men, a stick being a plane-load. At that time only Whitley bombers were being used to jump from. The Sergeant in charge was a trained Para and also a physical training instructor. He warned us that the work would become more difficult as the days progressed, until after two weeks we would be given tests to complete before we could have final acceptance for the Para course at Manchester. At any time we could call it a day, and return to our units with no ill feelings. All the training, though hard, was voluntary.

We still had no idea of what exactly was in store for us, but as the days went by we found that we had to do more and more, until we could hardly find the energy to go for a meal when the work was done. I had made up my mind to endure whatever was dealt out to me, and to complete the course. It became more strenuous every day, but we still had to run about the camp at all times.

First thing in the morning, we paraded in full battle dress with rifle and bayonet. Then we went on a forced march, that is, running for twenty minutes, walking very quickly for five, then running again. Hardwick was in the centre of a mining area of Derbyshire, with small villages every few miles, each with a coal mine. Our route would take us through Clay Cross, Pilesley, Shireland and Tibshelf, all quite near to Chesterfield. Each had its bakers' and butchers' shops, where the women would be queueing for rations. The names they called the Sergeant, as he shouted at us, were unrepeatable: they thought he was a 'Cruel, callous so-and-so!' You could see the horrified look on their faces if one of the lads had to be half-carried. Rather than let him down, his friends would help him to make it, carrying his rifle and helping him on the hills. It took me all my strength to carry my own kit, and I would not have been much help to anyone in trouble!

On arrival back at camp, we changed into PT dress, and carried out physical training till dinner time. The food was exceptionally good and we could have as much as we wanted. The extra rations which we enjoyed from now on were necessary to enable us to do the strenuous work, and it was quickly burned up. After the midday meal the routine would continue with the assault course. Five-gallon drums filled with earth would be carried about from one point to another, as we swung about on ropes and climbed between trees. By 4.30 it was time to collapse into bed absolutely exhausted.

I was still only seventeen years old, and I could feel the benefit of all the training, which built up my confidence in my ability to do what had seemed to be impossible only a week before. Some people could not stay the pace and left the camp very quickly. Once they had given up, they were quickly returned to units, as it was called, and about 30% could not make it and were RTU.

For those of us who succeeded, the next stop was Ringway, near Manchester. We left on a Sunday morning, so that the course in parachuting could begin on the Monday morning. The RAF accommodation was very good, and so was the cooking. Discipline there was much more relaxed. We found it easy to get on with the RAF instructors, who were all physical training instructors converted to parachuting. We stayed in our sticks of ten, and on the first day were introduced to the training hangar, with its circuit of swings and slides and, in one corner high in the roof, a platform to jump from, called the fan. What a grand bunch of chaps those RAF instructors were! They made everything enjoyable.

Behind glass windows along one side of the hangar, were dozens of WAAFs, all engaged in the packing of 'chutes on very long tables. Above the window was a notice in large print: DO NOT DISTRACT THE GIRL'S ATTENTION, SHE

COULD BE PACKING YOUR 'CHUTE. We never did.

On the runway stood five Whitley bombers converted for parachuting; a hole about a yard and a half across by less than a yard, in the middle of the fuselage, was our departure point. Before we attempted a jump, an old passenger 'plane with two very large engines was supposed to give us air experience. It was broken down while I was there, so I didn't get the benefit of the first flight before my first aircraft jump.

A lot of practice on the ground had to be completed before we even fitted a parachute. We learned how to take a fall along the body from the feet, the side of the leg, the body, and finally on to the back; spreading the weight of the body like this made it seem so easy. Later on, when fully trained, we would have to carry up to 80 pounds of equipment too. It was then that landing could be dangerous if the technique were not learned properly. The big swing we used, with a harness to sit in, was great fun. After we had been at Ringway a week, it was time to try a real jump.

The jumping area was a place eight miles away called Tatton Park. It was a lovely park, with a lake at one end and some very fine trees, in the centre of which was a huge grass area with a small road running through it. A balloon with a cage hanging below it was waiting to give us our first experience of the necessary height – our first two jumps would be made from it at 800 feet. It was 6am, because at that time of day the wind speed was usually below 15mph, as it had to be for safety. The cold, damp air made our task anything but inviting, but we were most surprised to see that the WVS had turned out to give us tea and a bun from their little mobile canteen.

One of the lads who came from Scotland at the same time as myself was called McPhee. He was a joker, and always had something to say. His remarks about the queer fastenings on the 'chute, such as 'What's this hanging down here? Looks like an old, well worn one to me', just as you were about to get into the cage for a jump, did nothing to steady your nerves. Four of us sat one in each corner, with our legs tucked into the side, leaving the hole clear in the bottom. The Sergeant stood to one side and we started the ascent. It took a few minutes to reach 800 feet, and the wind grew stronger. It whistled through the steel wires on the balloon. We were advised not to look down, so I concentrated on the balloon above, swinging us from side to side.

'Ready Number One,' came the command. 'Load and clear.'

I was Number Two; 'Go!' shouted the Sergeant. We waited for a second or two; a crack like a whip told us that Number One's 'chute had opened.

'Ready Number Two.' I swung my feet down into the hole. In no time I was falling. Hell! What an experience! I had a bit of a black-out, then a tug at my shoulders brought me back to life. It was fantastic, the adrenalin seemed to be bursting in my veins, the view was wonderful and I could see for miles. I was just beginning to relax when a voice from a loud-speaker below shouted, 'Get your feet together, Number Two.' The ground was coming up quickly now. Feet together, shoulders round, elbows in, head well forward, watch the ground: this drill had been hammered into us during training. Down I came for a forward landing to the right – beautiful! What a marvellous feeling it is to complete a jump – makes you feel on top of the world!

Soon the balloon was on its way up again, and this time I had a look at the tiny figures below. The Canteen had little, white specks around it: those who had jumped were looking up at us. I jumped as Number One, and the experience was the same but I kept my eyes open all the time, so I did not miss a thing. I watched the canopy come out of the pack on my back and develop into a beautiful 'chute above me. It was all over too quickly, for I would have loved to have spent a long time looking at the view.

Next day we took off in a Whitley bomber for our first aircraft jump. I had not been up in a 'plane before; it was most exciting to hear the roar of the engines as we sped down the runway. We sat five forward, and five behind the hole in the centre of the fuselage. There was less room toward the tail as the fuselage became smaller, and it meant sitting with knees up to chest. The 'chute was very bulky, making it difficult for a person with long legs to get comfortable. Fortunately it was only a few minutes before we reached the DZ (dropping zone). Only two men were dropped each time we crossed over the DZ before circling round again.

My turn came, and I went whizzing out of the hole; the slipstream caught me and I was carried away, and then once more I was dangling down and looking at a marvellous view. Before the 'plane came round again I had almost reached the canteen for a cup of tea that tasted out of this world.

The following day McPhee was jumping after me, as we had another jump in pairs before doing a jump with four, then eight altogether, which formed a stick in the sky all at once. I jumped, my 'chute opened beautifully, but McPhee came out very soon after me and dropped like a stone with his 'chute fluttering down above him: he had a crossed line, which stopped his canopy developing.

Only half an hour earlier he had said to me, 'That looks like a ropey old 'chute, hardly seems packed properly.' When I got out of mine, I ran towards him, but the ambulance which was always on standby had reached him first and was driving away.

Every day I called at the hospital on the Station, but they would not allow anyone to see him, they just said he was comfortable, and for 46 years I believed that he must have died, but an official report found in Brize Norton RAF Museum showed that he had fractured and crushed a vertebra. No further entries about him were made in the Station records for Course No. 59, April 1943.

In all we had to do eight jumps to qualify for our wings. One jump was in darkness from a balloon, and one was with all our equipment in battle order. The weapons and ammunition were loaded into containers six feet long and slung in the bomb bays of the aircraft, half-way through the stick. They would be released so that they would land between number five and six in the stick, and we would run and collect the weapons in order to go to war. Thank goodness, by the time I did go to war we used better methods.

In the middle of April 1943 we returned to Hardwick, this time to be posted to a battalion. The 1st Brigade were already fighting in North Africa. The 5th Scottish and the 6th Royal Welsh battalions would be leaving soon to join them, ready to invade Italy. My name was down for the Royal Welsh, and I now had a black flash hanging down from my collar at the back of my blouse, a relic from the days when wigs were worn in that regiment.

The brasses on our equipment had to be painted green, so as not to reflect the light, and 'khaki drill' clothing, or KD, was issued for Middle East service. When all this was sorted out, we were allowed two weeks' leave, which was called 'embarkation leave'.

At this stage my Mother had no idea that I had become an Airborne soldier, nor that I would be going to North Africa. My pay had been increased, to give me an extra fourteen shillings (jump pay). Seven shillings (35p) of this I allotted to my Mother. She liked my maroon beret and the nice blue wings I was wearing, in fact everything was all right until I mentioned North Africa. This caused so much upset that I

PARACHIUTE TRAINING SCHOOL RINGWAY
REPORT ON COURSE NO. 59

UNIT: PARACHUTE BRIGADE REINFORCEMENTS
                 and 30th COMMANDOS.
DATES: 5.4.43 - 16.4.43
NATURE OF COURSE: LONG COURSE (8 Jumps)
NUMBER OF DESCENTS Balloon   370)
                   Night Balloon 163)Total Descents:1,363
                   Aircraft   830)

1. Results

Intake		Qualified		Refusals		Misc		Injuries	
Offs	ORs	Offs	ORs	Offs	ORs	Offs	ORs	Offs	ORs
9	179	8	155	-	10	1	4	-	10
			+						

                     + 2 men recalled on authority of
Airborne Div.

PERCENTAGE OF FAILURES: 15.9

2. Conditions   WEATHER (AVERAGE WIND).
Average wind speed was 8-10 mph. The wind was generally
rather variable and gusty, otherwise weather conditions
were bright and sunny.

                     GROUND. Good conditions - dry
and firm.

3. Standard of Proficiency. SYNTHETIC. The course was
unimpressive in Ground Training and the standard was low at
the beginning, but improved to reach an average standard in
the end.

                     AIR JUMPS. Quite a good stan-
dard of jumping was reached, particularly on exit and
flight. The majority of pupils were soon 'turn conscious'
but their reactions on ground assessment and landings were
slow.

                     MORALE. Morale was high and
the men were cheerful and in good spirits throughout the
period of training.

4. General Remarks.   The course as a whole
achieved quite a good standard of parachuting ability. The
response from the pupils however was variable and there
were a considerable number of minor injuries. It is pointed
out that this course has again had only one week of training at Hardwicke and although they have been more carefully
selected than previous courses, the acceleration of the
training rather offsets the advantages of careful selec-
tion.

5. Appendix.
        A.   Nominal Roll of Those who Passed.
        B.   Nominal Roll of those Who Failed.
        C.   Separate List of Officers Who Passed.

NOMINAL ROLL OF OFFICERS AND OTHER RANKS WHO FAILED
TO COMPLETE THE 59th COURSE OF PARAHUTE TRAINING

UNIT: PARACHUTE BRIAGDE REINFORCEMENTS AND 30th COMMANDOS.

		PART1	No. of Descents		
REFUSALS (10)		CAUSE	Bln.	N.Bln.	A/C
3244103	Pte Torrance	No apparent cause. Refused on ground.	2	–	2
5948503	afm Ewer	Performing well until refusal. Stated nervousness as cause.	2	1	3
3311837	Pte Wardill	Not a good performer and poor physique. Said he couldn't make it.	2	1	3
1026022318	Pte Wall	A good performer. Domestic influence stated as reason.	2	1	4
2766533	Pte Horton	Refused to draw chute for his 5th A/C. His friend was seriously injured the day before.	2	1	4
3976518	Pte Egnon	Refused to draw chute for his NB descent.	2	–	2
3970363	Pte Howell	Refused to draw chute for his NB descent.	2	–	2
3975403	Pte Wood	Refused to continue jumping when fit after injury.	2	–	1
5773076	Pte Hall	Refused on 2nd A/C. Said he was nervous and could not swing his legs into aperture for stick jumping.	2	–	1
5783190	Pte Cole	Refused on 2nd A/C. Said he was unable to carry on as he was too nervous. Inclined to be awkward.	2	–	1

		PART II			
MISCELLANEOUS (5)		CAUSE			
251293	2/Lt Rolington	Unsuitable on GT refused to make fan descent. very nervous. RTU.	–	–	–
4617131	Pte Cadman	Road accident - did not jump. Found unsuitable on GT. When fit RTU.	–	–	–
5569893	Pte Dyer	Unsuitable on GT. Refused to make a fan descent. RTU.	–	–	–
3782726	Sig Hales	Severe cold. Hospital.	–	–	–
3976282	Pte Neagle	Strained Rectus abdominis muscle - hospital.	–	–	–

10602440	Pte	Seaman	Cheerful And a good performer.
14311518	Pte	Schermuly	VG performer. Excellent in every way. V strongly recommended.
14206353	Pte	Smith	Performance quite good and has worked well.
3971348	Cpl	Stocks	Acted as stick leader and has done the job well.
6852086	LCpl	Stevens	A good type, has jumped well at times.
6214133	Rfm	Shelley	A good type has reached a good standard in stick work.
3603398	Fus	Sherlock	A cheerful fearless type who has done well on all jumps.
3136119	Fus	Sweeney	Has made satisfactory progress, average type.
3975196	Pte	Samuel	An average type, has made satisfactory progress.
5671975	Pte	Scott	Rather nervous. Has shown improvement
3976126	Pte	Sullivan	A keen and confident jumper, good type.
3975558	Pte	Selby	A good jumper, confident and keen, has jumped well.
5508116	Cpl	Toogood	A satisfactory performance.
14311521	Tpr	Thompson	Good performer - lacks enthusiasm.
14221210	Pte	Taylor	Lacks concentration but tries hard. Good worker.
46125523	Pte	Tetley	Started off badly but has progressed.
14215826	Pte	Tucker	Lacking in body control but keen and confident.
6204431	Pte	Unwin	Cheerful And a good performer.
2613	Pte	Verstracten	Very good with cheerful manner. Confident and very good jumper.
6205172	Pte	Wakeling	Has shown real interest and jumped well.
3663637	Pte	Wilson	A very good performance.
3461289	Pte	Wallace	Has worked hard and performed well.
132433	Pte	Ware	A good performance part from bad landing on 3rd A/C.
10602382	Pte	Worthington	Keen and a good performer.
3197481	Pte	Wells	Has good qualities for NCO. Performed well.
6087069	Sgt	Wilkinson	Very good man. Strongly recommended.
4345732	Cpl	Wilson	Very good man. Confident and enthusiastic jumper. Good leader.
2606377	Pte	Wells	Worked hard, very keen and good at stick jumping.
14203183	Pte	Watson	Very good worker and good team man in stick jumping. Very good.
4617157	Pte	Wall	A surly type but has worked well. Rather slow.
3975544	Pte	Walsh	Has worked well throughout the course. Has jumped well.
4341427	Sgt	Young	Average on ground training but a good performer in the aircraft and in the air.
3192209	LCpl	Wilson	Injured shoulder on last jump. VG performer.
3532235	Pte	Byrne	Performed well and reliable type.
5623005	Pte	Beesley	A good performance. Steady type.
6205026	Cpl	Edwards	Keen and capable.
643676	Sgt.	Door	A good performer.
6007799	Pte	England	Injury delayed completed, good all round performance.
1470451	Pte	Colvin	A good type, keen and confident, jumped well.

14401954	Pte McClusky	A good type, has done well throughout course.
3993374	Pte Bradley	Slight injury delayed completion of course. A good pupil and excellent performer.
5511303	L/C Taylor	Jumping delayed by slight injury. Otherwise a satisfactory performance.
5670996	LSgt Loader	Not very confident for an NCO. Slow on exits. Tries hard.

PART III

INJURIES (10)		Nature	Cause	A.	B.	C.
6215595	Pte Aldens	Sprained ankle.	Slid forward with weight on one foot.1st A/C.		B.	
3250168	Sgt Witten	Concussion	Failed to hold a turn on 2nd A/C descent.			C.
6209741	Pte Smith	Concussion	Failed to turn 2nd A/C descent.		B.	
14403005	Pte McPhee	Crushed vertebra fracture.	Heavy landing following thrown line and incomplete development of canopy.			C.
6924766	Sig Evans	Sprained shoulder	Heavy landing on shoulder on GT.		B.	
4124336	L/C Whittaker	Strained abdominal muscles	Old injury during training at Hardwicke.		B.	
2925195	Pte Green	Sprained ankle	Landed on very rough ground		B.	
5771700	Pte Glover	Concussion	Delayed effect of heavy landing.		B.	
5672241	Cpl Hinton	Injured knee	Heavy landing on 1st A/C.		B.	
4615410	Cpl Goddard	Concussion	Failed to release turn and landed heavily on back.		B.	

A.	up to 2 days	)	
B.	2 to 7 days	)	disability
C.	7 days and over	)	

From: Parachute Training School, Royal Air force, Ringway.

To: Headquarters No 70 Group
         Copies to: Headquarters Army Co-operation Command
                    Headquarters Airborne Division
                    Headquarters 2nd Parachute Brigade
                    Headquarters 3rd Parachute Grigade

Date: 26 April 1943

Ref: PTS/S2/6/Air

Parachute Training
Reports on Courses - Airborne division
Attachments - Course 59

The following who failed to complete their parachute training on their oroginal course were attached to the 59th
Course to complete to complete the required number of
descents.

				No. of Descents		
From 55th Course				Bln.N	Bln.A/C	
Cpt		Rigby-Jones	Completed Average parachuting standard.	2	–	2
2/Lt		Roberts	Completed	–	–	1
Attached from 58th course						
14370590	Spr	Adams	Very good all round performer	2	1	5
5344504	Rfm	Jackson	Hard worker but could improve. Inclined to be nervous.	2	1	5
10602289	Pte	Spencer	V good performer and keen.	2	1	5

Signed: JC KILKENNY
Suqadron Leader Commanding
Parachute Training School
ROYAL AIR FORCE RINGWAY

wished I had kept my mouth shut, but the damage was done. I was very sorry to see her so troubled, but I thought at that time that she would soon get over it.

Two days after I had reported back to Hardwick, the CO sent for me. I could not imagine what he would want with me; I knew I had not been in any trouble. All the lads in my company were just as anxious as I. The RSM, Jerry Strachan, marched me into the CO's office; I stood to attention, the RSM was dismissed, and I was told to pull a chair up. My thoughts were running riot. The CO started by asking my age.

'Nineteen', I replied straight away.

I could tell that he did not believe me, and wondered how he could have found out. He had been in action at Dunkirk, and went on to tell me that it was not all that it was cracked up to be, and should be avoided if at all possible. Within days, he said, the Brigade would be in action, and he had this proposal to put to me: 'How would you like to have another two weeks' leave and join the 6th Airborne, now forming at Salisbury?'

'No, Sir,' I replied, 'I would rather go to North Africa.'

He would not take this as my final answer: he said to think it over, and come back at 4pm. He also said I would make new friends with my new unit, and would have every opportunity to see action when the invasion of Europe took place.

'The RSM will have a railway warrant and a leave pass ready if you will accept, and we will send you to join the 6th Airborne. You should have at least another year's training in this country before the Second Front opens.'

When I got back to the billet my friends wanted to know what had been said. When I told them, 'Well, what are you waiting for? Get going on leave!'

I told them I had refused, and that did it. I was called by all the names they could think of; they never let up from then on, I was completely browbeaten all day, and at 4pm I was marched once more into the CO's office.

'Well, what's it going to be?'

'Leave', I said.

'You have made a very wise decision, and I wish you the very best of luck and a successful career in the 6th Airborne Division.'

The lads I had trained with left for North Africa and joined the 1st Division. The 6th Battalion later sailed in HMS *Abdiel* from Bizerta, to occupy Taranto in Italy. HMS *Abdiel* was blown up by a mine and sank in two minutes. Lots of boys were drowned.

By 5pm I was standing on the station at Chesterfield with another leave pass in my hand. It was years before I learned what had happened. My Mother had told our Vicar, Mr. Townsley. He was an old soldier and knew just what to say: at

```
C. in C. Mediterranean, Sept. 1943. (Case 7588)

10th Sept, 1943 (Page 69)
11.CASUALTIES
ABDIEL sank in Taranto harbour as a result of an
explosion which occurred at 0015. The ship was at
anchor and the explosion is believed to have been
caused by a German "S" type mine. The ship promptly
broke in two and sank in two minutes. Casualties
amongst the ship's company were surprisingly small but
the 400 troops on board suffered very heavy casualties
and considerable stores, M/T and guns were lost.
```

seventeen I should not have been in the Army at all, never mind going overseas into action. He had seen me confirmed by the Bishop of Whitby only four years earlier; nevertheless, he himself joined the Army under age during the Great War, so he must have had some sympathy for me.

During this leave period I took a girl I knew called Dorothy home to meet my parents. We had been friends since we were fifteen years old. It was not a very successful experience; in fact later that week, as a result, she told me that she did not think we had a future together, and that we were very young to be getting so serious and should give ourselves some time to think about it, so we said goodbye to each other.

Middlesbrough did not get any serious attention from the Luftwaffe, but the odd 'plane that did find its way there caused quite a lot of damage. The day after my Father saw me off at the station, a lunch-time train was hit, putting the service out for several days.

Dorothy was living in a house close to where a bomb was dropped in July 1942, No. 25 Albert Terrace to be precise. Her father had erected an Anderson shelter in the back garden, and had piled soil on top of it. I was told that during the raid, her family had dashed down into the shelter and she picked up a coat in the dark as she passed through the hall. It was not until the candles were lit inside the shelter that her mother saw that it was her own best fur coat, and she was not very pleased!

A loud whistle had saved Dorothy from a scolding, and as everyone crouched down the bomb landed on No. 35 with a tremendous thud. Soil came in through the joints of the Anderson and the door was blown away. No. 35 was a heap of rubbish and one of Dorothy's friends was killed at only sixteen years old. On duty as an air-raid warden, Dorothy's father had been standing on the front steps of No. 25; the blast had flung him along the hall. Luckily he was only shaken, but his small dog never recovered from the shock, and he died. In the next street several houses had been hit and a sailor, home on leave, was killed as part of the road lifted up and covered him.

Shops at the corner of Clifton Street and Victoria Road were badly damaged. Every window in the area was blown out, and horrible black soot from coal fires, which were used in those days, came down the chimneys and covered everything. Pots fell from shelves and ornaments were smashed, and curtains hung drunkenly from gaping windows, having been hit by flying glass. It was a very frightening experience for people in that area, but those safely in shelters had survived. No. 35 was at the corner of Albert Terrace, where we used to kiss goodnight; however that was all over now and we each went our own way.

Chapter 4

Training at Bulford and Netheravon

The following months were spent on Salisbury Plain at Bulford Camp, the home of the 6th Airborne Division during the war years. I had joined the 9th Battalion; there were only 200 men in it to start with but new members turned up every day. The barracks were very good and were in what was called the Sandhurst block, which had a first floor. The weather seemed always to be fine, which was just as well, as we spent little time in the barracks. Every hour was occupied with outdoor schemes, training, training and more training. The Battalion was taking shape and comradeship developing, as we shared the hardships presented on exercises spent moving about the South of England through rivers, woods and valleys.

Lieutenant-Colonel Martin Linsay, the CO, or Polar Joe, as we called him, because he wore the white ribbon of the Polar Medal for his work in the 1930s, said that a contingent of men were due to arrive in Bulford from India. Those who wished could welcome them to the Battalion. He marched quite a large party of us to the station. About 30 soldiers got off the train, and the Colonel knew just about all of them. Some wore Australian bush hats, but all had their Para wings. They had trained in India.

They all had the Indian Frontier medal, and had seen peacetime service as regulars. The only names I can remember are Rose and Luke, who both became corporals within weeks of joining 'C' Company. We young soldiers were amazed when they pulled white sheets from their kitbags, and dressed in pyjamas. They were all much older than us and had so many interesting yarns about India, which they told as we sat around their beds or in the NAAFI. They introduced us to Hindustani, and very soon we had new names for everything. The white sheets did not last long, as we did not have a 'dhobi wallah' in Bulford. Then they just used the four rough blankets like us. During training we noticed they were not as fit as we were, so they must have had a soft life in India. They quickly improved: they had to!

More recruits joined the 9th Para, and soon we had reached our full strength of over 600. The Colonel was not always with us on the training schemes, and Major Otway, his Second in Command, would lead us. He eventually was promoted and became the CO. After the war, Martin Linsay became Sir Martin Linsay, MP.

RAF Netheravon was our local air field, just a couple of miles away from the camp. Regularly, we would take off during late evening, and drop miles away. The exercises would last four days, during which time we would get very little or no sleep. We would march and run for miles, to end up back at the barracks. There was always plenty of hot water in the showers and good food waiting for us, and we would spend the following day cleaning all the equipment and would have everything spruced up ready for inspection.

On Saturday morning the CO would make his rounds; then by lunch time we would be off to London on a 36-hour pass, and by 2pm the train would be arriving in Waterloo Station. Most of the lads lived in the London area, and special trains, all arriving within a few minutes, brought the whole Division on weekend leave every two weeks. The same trains would return at 11pm on Sunday evening, and the Waterloo area would be a sea of maroon berets. We all had to be back by one minute to midnight, and we usually were.

Within two days, preparation would be going on for the next exercise. This would be carried out on the following weekend and on into the next week. Then once again we would receive our leave passes and be off to the capital. My first call used to be at the Red Shield Club, run by the Salvation Army; for 1/9d (8 pence) a bed and breakfast could be booked. Several clubs, the Union Jack Club and the Stage Door Canteen, also the Nuffield Centre, were all free to enter and the food was reasonably priced, which was just as well, as I never had enough money to pay for food, and could not afford to go to the pictures. We needed the very good food that we got at Bulford, as we burned it up very quickly.

I thoroughly enjoyed my weekends in London. I would walk for miles, developing a healthy appetite, so I spent every penny I had on food. After a few visits there I found my way around the whole central area, from London Bridge to Chelsea, Marble Arch to King's Cross, Oxford Street, the Strand, Leicester Square and Piccadilly, Whitehall and

Victoria. I located the famous museums and Madame Tussauds, but unfortunately they were always closed on Sundays.

One Sunday morning, while on a visit to the Zoo in Regent's Park, I entered the Parrot House, which was a long building, just as two girls were leaving by the door at the far end, and a large bird coloured red and green made the whole place echo with a very loud wolf whistle. The girls turned round and gave me a nasty look, but I did not expect much else from them in London. They all had eyes only for the thousands of Yanks, who had so much money to throw around.

I did get involved with one American, who approached me with two heavily painted women, one on each arm. He wanted me to join the party and, when I quickly explained that I had no money, 'Don't worry about that,' he said, 'we are going for a meal and it's on me.' We walked into a smart restaurant in Piccadilly, and after a lovely meal and drinks he paid for it from a whole roll of notes. With the generous tip he gave the waiters alone, I could have had a grand time. It soon became clear to me that the women were gold-diggers who were only after his money, and at the age of seventeen I thought it repulsive. When we left the restaurant just before midnight, I made some excuse about having to be back in the barracks, and cleared off to my bed in the Salvation Army Canteen.

A month later I found my name on a list to attend a special course in London on German army vehicles. It was top secret and I had no idea what was involved, but reported to a garage in North Finchley. At ground level it looked like an ordinary garage, but in the basement there was every kind of German vehicle, which must have come from North Africa.

There were ten of us on the course, billeted in private houses close by. I was sent to a fairly large house, to live with a bank manager and his family. We reported to the garage each morning at 8am and worked until 5pm. The object was for us to learn how to mobilise demobilised vehicles. An Airborne unit relies on capturing enemy transport, and German transport was always immobilised when not in use. We had to be familiar with all types of engines, even in motor cycles, and with making rotor arms with bits of brass strips and hose pipe. We learned how to break doors quickly and start the engines without ignition keys, noting the different firing sequences of the trucks and cars. After two weeks we could have an engine running in 25 seconds, even though the rotor arm had been missing, and the distributor disconnected from the plug leads.

The bank manager had two daughters, both a few years older than me, and one night I returned to find them upset. Both their boyfriends were in the Services and had been expected home the next Saturday for a 36-hour pass. Seats had been booked for the Savoy Theatre in the Strand, but one of them could not come home. It must have occurred to them that I was available, and I was asked if I would make up a foursome. When the other boyfriend arrived, he proved to be a captain in the Engineers, but he was quite friendly and never pulled rank on me.

Having accepted, I realised that I only had my second-best battledress with me, which was passable but not nearly as smart as my best one. We left Finchley by tube for the West End, and soon we were taking our seats in the Circle at the Savoy. The girls wore evening dress and the Captain wore his field service uniform and his Sam Brown belt, and I could not help feeling scruffy as I sat with them.

The show was called *My Sister Eileen*; it was a new experience for me as I had never been to a theatre before, and I enjoyed it very much. At half-time we visited the bar and had a sherry and soon the bell warned us to return to our seats for the second half. I had never rubbed shoulders with so many toffs before.

The show over, we made our way down to the Savoy Hotel intending to have a meal; the Captain must have been loaded. We left our berets and the belt at the cloak room, and I just had time to see mine put in a pigeon hole beside a hat with so much 'scrambled egg' on it, it must have belonged to an admiral. Others I saw had red bands round them, denoting staff officers' rank in the Army. The head waiter eyed me up and down and I felt that at any moment he would ask me to leave. He went away and came back full of apologies, as he could not find an empty table. I felt relieved, as this was no place for me to sit in comfort.

It was decided to go down to Lyons' Corner House, and in the basement we found a much nicer atmosphere; the band was playing, the food was excellent and served with great courtesy. Almost everyone was in uniform, with servicemen who had come from all over the world. My only expense was two shillings, which I tipped the doorman for finding a taxi for us.

I took badly to hard training again after this little holiday. We started on a new scheme which meant we would be working during the night for a week. Our days started at 6pm with breakfast, then there was weapon training, even shooting in the dark. We had to prime grenades with detonators, strip machine-guns and load the magazines in total darkness, until we could do it as quickly and accurately and efficiently as in daylight. At midnight we had our main meal, and tea was at 4.30am, after which we could leave the camp if we wanted to. The day was our own till 6pm when we started work again. At 9am I would take the 'bus into Salisbury, which I had not seen in daylight before, take a look at the shops and visit the Cathedral, before returning to camp for some sleep before 6pm. This suited me well: it was a complete change in routine, and as good as a rest!

Cross-country runs were held as often as possible, and I suppose it was noted that I could run. Two soldiers and an NCO from each battalion had to report to Netheravon to fly to Scotland and take part in some games held at the Polish Brigade camp. Gus Gower, Sergeant McGeaver and I reported, having been chosen, and we joined some lads from the 7th and 8th Battalions and the 1st Canadian Para. A Whitley landed, and carried us off to Leuchars in Fife. Trucks were waiting, and took us through St Andrews and along the Fife coast to Largo House, Headquarters of the Polish Brigade. We were met by their CO and made very welcome, and then introduced to their Sergeants' Mess, where we could eat and also be waited on. We could not believe our luck, at the prospect of this seven days' holiday!

We took part in shooting, grenade throwing and bayonet fencing competitions, but we did not win anything, since the Poles were much better than us. However, Gus Gower and I found that the NAAFI girls liked to hear English boys talking, after dealing with the Poles for so long, and we could not do anything wrong as far as they were concerned. We took them to dances and spent a lot of time in the canteen; in fact we just helped ourselves to what we wanted and did not have to pay for a thing.

It was great to be back in Scotland and hear all the familiar terms I had learned in Aberdeen. On the day before we went back to Bulford it was a Saturday, and before the football match began at Upper Largo we all had to march on to the centre of the football pitch. The Polish Ambassador came and spoke to us, and then the band played our national anthem. We were very sorry to say goodbye to Largo, when the 'plane which had brought us took us back to Netheravon and back to the grind again.

We were building up to another big exercise, however, and soon were going back up to Scotland again. This time the whole 9th Battalion flew from Netheravon in Whitleys, and were to jump in front of some VIP's, who inspected them prior to partaking in a scheme involving mountain troops, on the mountains near Granton on Spey. The 'planes made for a point just north of London, and then followed the railway line over Peterborough, Doncaster, York and Darlington. There were no windows in the 'plane but, looking through a rivet hole in the fuselage, I could see the ICI plant smoking away over Teesside, and felt a bit homesick, being so near yet not being able to call. Soon we crossed the coast east of Edinburgh and went out to sea. An hour later we turned to run in over the Spey estuary and the covers over the hole in the floor were opened. I was keen to get out, but also very stiff, since we had been flying for four hours. Whitleys did not much exceed 100mph flat out.

The red light came on and we shuffled along towards the aperture; green on, and we started to jump. Soon it was my turn, and it was lovely to feel the fresh air on my face and hear the noise of the engine fade away as I came down. It was a beautiful afternoon in August, the sun shone on the river Spey below, and the scenery was magnificent.

Two lads landed in the river, but managed to scramble to the bank. My friend Gus Gower burned his face on the static line and was taken to Aberdeen Hospital. Everyone else lined up before a group of high-ranking officers from Norway, Denmark and the British Army, and questions were asked about the equipment we used and some of our weapons which had not been seen before outside the Airborne forces. Paratroops had only been formed two years ago, but already had made an impact in North Africa.

We marched into Granton on Spey and were allocated some empty houses to sleep in. The house used by my company seemed a bit cramped, so three of us occupied a very large dog kennel. It had plenty of straw in it, and was very comfortable.

Trucks arrived from the Lovat Scouts to take us to a demonstration of their equipment. They had been trained as mountain troops. Shortly they would be leaving to take up positions on Ben Macdhui, the second highest mountain in Scotland. We were to follow them the next day and try to attack their position, though it was thought unlikely that we would succeed, since we had never done any climbing before or had any training in mountain warfare. They considered that it would take us 48 hours to reach the top of the mountain.

Next morning we made our way to Aviemore and along a track towards Cairn Gorm, which had to be climbed first before we could attempt Ben Macdhui. I found it very hard going, carrying a Bren machine-gun and four magazines with 28 rounds in each, plus all my equipment and a full water bottle. Every half hour we rested for five minutes, during which we had to take off all our gear, put on a warm pullover and then repack it, dress and move on. The wind was getting stronger as we gained height, and it was quite cold by the time we had reached 2,000 feet (600m). It was already midday, and we were beginning to think that the Lovat Scouts were right about it taking us two days to get to reach the top.

By dusk it was raining and we still had not reached 4,000 feet. The wind was so strong that we could lean on it without falling over, and rocks the size of a table made the going slow; we had to jump from one to another, which was very awkward in the failing light. We reached smaller stones, which made it easier, just as the snow came lashing into us in the strong wind. It was still 250 feet to the summit, and we had to move very slowly indeed, since we had been warned of a 200-foot drop from a ledge at one point.

Word came that we had made contact with the Lovat Scout positions. We waited till a forward patrol had located all of them, in little bunkers which they had built from the plentiful supply of rocks in the area to shelter them from the gale, which was now at full force on top of the mountain. Moving up, we took up positions near them, with fixed bayonets pointing at their throats. When the CO fired an illuminating flare, lighting up the area, the Jocks could not believe it: they had expected us about lunch time the next day, especially with such a gale blowing up. We got down alongside of them with our gas capes on; these were kind of oilskin coats, and we slept in them till 5am, though we were still frozen and wet through. I thought, 'If this is mountain warfare, they can keep it!'

The scheme was now over, so we made our way down the south side of the mountain towards the Lin of Dee, near Braemar. The streams were in full spate after the storm, from the water that came rushing down the hills. We had been told to follow the water to the bottom of the hills, and the streams became small rivers as the lower heights were reached. Soon the tops of the trees came up out of the mists, and lower down we passed through a pine forest and could see the river Dee below. Down on the road was a line of trucks waiting to take us to Braemar.

Even though wet through, tired, hungry and feeling pretty miserable, I could not take my eyes off the scenery. The views of the countryside were wonderful. The grass was a beautiful green, and the pine trees gave off their lovely smell in the morning air. The mountains disappeared into the mist at about 1000 feet, and it was still raining, but everything looked fresh and beautiful. I decided that one day, if I survived the war, I would come back here, and perhaps then I could enjoy the beauty of it all at leisure.

The Fife Arms was base camp for the Commandos; they were out on an exercise, so we were able to use their facilitiess. There was plenty of hot water, and we were able to put our gear in the large boiler house to dry out, while we had a good sleep after a grand meal.

Our own transport had arrived from Bulford with our best battle dress and boots. We handed in our smocks and equipment in exchange, so that we could smarten ourselves up ready for a march through Aberdeen, and a church parade. It was great to see the city again. I was able to call in at the driving school to say 'Hello' to my instructors. We left by train for Edinburgh, where we were guests of the Lord Provost. Special buses with open tops took us round the city, and girls in windows above knitwear factories threw sweets and cigarettes down into the 'buses. A meal had been arranged in Redfern Barracks, where the Royal Scots stationed there waited at table for us! This was unheard of: before we had always had to queue for meals, and only sergeants and above were waited on.

Our next stop was to be London, and after a march there each of us would receive a pass for ten days. It was silly for me to travel so close to home only to come travelling back again in another four hours. They gave me my pass at Edinburgh, so I jumped off the train at Darlington.

I met a friend of Ron Sturdy's, whose name was Norman Parr. He had made himself known to me when the 12th Battalion had been showing the flag in Middlesbrough, as they were all ex-Green Howards, which was the local regiment, and we became good friends. His mother gave a party in their home, which necessitated a look round town for some girls to take. In Marks and Spencer we came across two pretty girls who were serving at the counter, and asked them if they would like to come to the party. They agreed, and turned out to be very good company, and we took them to a dance or two before our leave was finished, but we did not write to them, so we cannot have been impressed.

Norman's battalion, the 12th Para, was stationed about a mile away from mine. After I had said goodbye to my parents once again, we returned together to Bulford camp.

Chapter 5

More Training in the 6th Airborne

In September the Yanks supplied us with C47 Dakotas. We used them for a drop before an exercise involving the Brigade, that is, the three battalions: the 8th and 9th and the 1st Canadian Parachute Battalions.

The Americans were used to dropping their own Para from 1,000 feet (300m), because the extra height was needed to use the reserve 'chutes which they always carried. We too were dropped at 1,000 feet, and a good job too, as you will learn. The Dakotas were great aircraft, far superior in every way to the Whitleys; we even had seats on each side of the 'plane to sit facing each other, and when standing up there was plenty of room for us to move toward the large door. We had practised jumping from the doorway. A wire ran from one end of the 'plane to the other above our heads, to clip our static lines on to before jumping. These lines ran smoothly, and well out of the way of any equipment.

Leaving Netheravon one night, we made toward the Yeovil area of Somerset. As we approached the DZ, we could tell by the engine noise that we had not slowed down, as was the practice with RAF pilots. They would have throttled back to about 90mph, but the Dakotas were doing twice that speed. The green light came on above the door, and we jumped.

The slipstream was so strong that it threw me against the other side of the door with a terrific crash. I lost control of my jumping position, which it is very important to keep in order to ensure a well done parachute exercise; my arms and legs were flying in all directions instead of being tight together, and my right foot caught in the rigging lines. I was coming down with my head where my feet should be.

It was pitch dark, so I had no idea how far I was from the ground, and the only thing I could do was to kick and kick and pull, which I did frantically but, no matter how I tried, my foot was fast in the lines. If only it had been in daylight, I would have seen what the matter was and put it right, and also would have known how much time I had to do it in. The ground must be coming up any second! Thoughts were running through my head like lightning: I must get my foot free or it was chips for me. In desperation I made a terrific struggle, kicking like hell, and all at once out it came. Two seconds later I was on the ground and, although it was a heavy landing, I did not hurt myself or do any damage. My thigh was painful from the bash against the door, however, and this made walking difficult.

The drop had been a shambles. We had been dropped in the wrong place, with the lads scattered over miles, due to the speed of the aircraft. Casualties were well above normal, in fact the scheme had to be cancelled the following day, instead of being run over the four days which had been planned. An umpire saw me limping and made me a casualty, pinning a card to my uniform. The medics arrived in a jeep and took me away, just as though it had been the real thing. I was very glad to rest the thigh: the blue bruising is still visible to this day, nearly 50 years on.

We noticed that in our recent schemes we had usually dropped 30 or 40 miles inland, and always made for the coast before the exercise was ended, finishing up at places like Poole, Weymouth, Bournemouth or Southampton. It was said that we would be used in this way for an operation either before or after the Second Front opened. We expected to be picked up by landing craft or submarine and brought home after completing the job.

Once the coastal point was reached the scheme would be over, and the sea was the obvious place for us all to cool off. The beaches down south were all cordoned off, with barbed wire in places, but we were not deterred, even though the shingle made our feet sore. I remember getting to the sea on my knees, keeping my blistered feet clear of the stones, as we had marched 50 miles across country during the previous 48 hours. Once in the water it was heaven for all our aching muscles as we just let the waves wash over our tired limbs. The company cooks set up hot meals in camping stoves, and we had a good meal before returning to Bulford. It must have rained at some time, but I don't remember the weather being anything but perfect during 1943.

The RAF took over flying the Dakotas from the Americans, and what a difference that made! The speed was cut down to 120mph and we were taken to the right places and dropped at

600 feet. It was a wonderful sight to see the Brigade drop, with about 30 Dakotas flying over the DZ at the same time. Everyone had completed route marches of 50 miles in full kit and was trained to perfection in field craft and weapon training. The comradeship in the unit was fantastic.

During our exercises we passed through some lovely villages in the South of England. There were times when we needed our water bottles filled, but few if any of the villagers would allow us to speak to them. Doors would be shut and curtains drawn quickly as we appeared, for no reason that we could think of. At times like these I missed my friends in Aberdeen.

In October I was detailed to collect a three-ton truck and take it, with a corporal and six lads, to a place in Rutlandshire called Uppingham. Rutland was the smallest county in England at that time. The land around was quite flat and mainly agricultural. The 1st Airborne Division were coming home from North Africa and Italy, and our job was to help get the accommodation ready in large houses taken over by the War Office. From a store we collected beds, blankets, tables, chairs etc., taking them to each of the houses, which were usually in their own grounds, with stables. Some of the houses and halls around Oakham in Leicestershire still had their owners living in one or two rooms with their staff. On one occasion a butler came out in his evening dress and asked us to make less noise. I often wondered what would happen when 100 or so lads were billeted there!

After duty we found a canteen in Uppingham village, used by the Land Army girls in the area. We had never seen so many girls! In Bulford there were only 60 or so girls working in the canteens, to 7,000 airborne troops, while here there must have been fifteen girls and only seven of us, with not a Yank in sight. I think the land girls were pleased to see some young blood, after working on the farms with farmers who were mainly old. They all lived in a hostel a mile out of town. A dance was planned for the following evening in the local church hall, and we were all invited. Next day we had to dash around at the double getting the work done. It would take us two weeks, well into November, before it was completed.

The dance was in full swing when we arrived, with the band consisting of a piano, some drums and a violin: they made a nice noise anyway. I was hopeful, if not hopeless, at dancing, but I found I was in great demand. There must have been three girls to every man, and we could not believe our luck. I met a very nice girl called Joan, who was quite tall. I was not usually attracted to tall girls, but she was so interesting to talk to that we got along fine. We went to the pictures the following week and she took me back to supper. They could invite guests back to the hostel, providing the supervisor approved of the choice of friend invited. We regularly met the girls in the canteen after duties, as there was nowhere else to go in Uppingham.

The night before we left I had to take the truck to the station at Oakham for 11pm. A train-load of lads was expected, and all transport had to be ready to take them to the various addresses where we had been stocking up. It was almost 10pm and I took all the girls back to their hostel, and then dashed off for the station appointment. The road was very narrow and twisting, and the time was getting on. There was a car in front which I could not get past; then I saw a straight stretch of road ahead, dropped into third gear and shot past the car, just managing to arrive at the station with five minutes to spare.

Suddenly the car I had passed on the road pulled up in front of me, and out stepped General Browning, Number One in the Airborne. He was meeting the train to welcome the boys back from North Africa. He was in his British warm overcoat, and highly polished riding boots. I could see that he was making straight for me.

'You the driver of this truck?'

'Yes, sir', I replied, frozen to the spot.

He stood tapping his leg with his riding crop as he continued, 'You must have been doing 50mph when you passed my driver. He could not keep up with you. I have never seen such driving in a three-ton truck in my life.'

My thoughts were already of the 'glasshouse' where, according to what I had heard, life was not worth living: it was just pure hell from morning till night.

At last he turned away; then suddenly he came back. I was still stood to attention, and in a different kind of voice, almost friendly, he said, 'I must admit you are a bloody good driver', and off he went leaving me sighing with relief. Everyone around dashed over to ask what he had said. Very few people got to speak to Boy Browning: usually they only listened.

Back in Bulford it was training, forever training, all over again.

My friend, Gus Gower, told me that he had spent twelve months in a correction camp when he was sixteen. He had been made to wheel barrow-loads of rubble into the Wash in

Norfolk, reclaiming land. I don't know what he had been up to, but he did not appear to have had a very happy childhood. He had once lived in the East End of London but after the bombing he had been moved to Canvey Island in the Thames. I was curious to know just where it was, and he suggested that I might go home with him on our next 36-hour leave pass. Gus was a very generous lad and was always interesting in conversation, and we got on well together.

We left from Liverpool Street Station for Canvey Island, which lies a few stops before Southend. We made our way across a bridge which, when the tide was in, was underwater, making it an island cut off from the mainland. In 1943 all the buildings there seemed to be of corrugated sheeting. Gus had told me that most were occupied by homeless people from the bombed area of London. Gus's house was a bungalow type of building.

We did not get a very good welcome on arrival: there did not seem to be anything to eat when he opened a cupboard and soon afterwards his mother told us there was nothing anywhere in the house. So Gus said, 'Come on, Ron, we will go down the café; they will have some beans on toast for us.'

That night there was a dance on in the church hall and, when it was in full swing, the air-raid siren went, and shortly afterwards all the lights went out. A gun battery just down the road opened fire, searchlights were lighting the area up, and the 'planes passed over on their way to London. They used to follow the Thames until they found the docks. The dance did not continue; it was about 11pm and everyone had gone home. I had lost Gus in the hall when the lights went out and was roaming around looking for him. I could not tell one building from another, as they were all in rows and of the same size and type.

A voice suddenly said, 'Is that you, Ron? Where have you been?' Gus struck a match and opened a door in one building, and we soon came upon the bedroom. His two young brothers were in the bed and we had to get in alongside of each of them. The children did not wake, but it was very cold. I pulled the blanket over my legs, then it was pulled off me as Gus got in the other side. This tugging went on until I decided to get dressed and lie on top of the bed. Then I started hunting for the toilet, but Gus said, 'Oh, just open the window, Ron.' So I did.

Next morning we woke to find the children gone; in fact there was no-one in the house at all. Gus had another idea, and took me down to the Ack-ack Station to scrounge a meal. This was at 9am on Sunday morning! Guarding the camp gates were two ATS girls with pickaxe handles. They shouted to the Guard Commander, who appeared from the guard room and said he was sure the cook would be able to fix us up, and we could go down to the kitchen. A friendly ATS sergeant put a large frying pan on the stove with two eggs, bacon and fried bread in it. We were made very welcome and I think the girls would have liked us to stay on, but it was pointless waiting for the later trains, which would be very crowded, and we wanted to be back in Bulford in reasonable time.

It had been an experience, seeing how Gus spent his weekends. I could not help but like the lad who was willing to share what he had with me. If only I had lived closer to Bulford, he could have come home with me and had a much better time on our 36-hour passes. The welcome I got when I went on leave was so different, and my parents would have made sure he had the best of whatever was going in the way of food and comfort.

It was almost Christmas by now. We could have either Christmas or New Year passes. Joan wrote and arranged for me to go to a party with her at New Year. The dance was very good, and the place was full of Ist Division Para lads; I had no idea that most of them would be dead by the same time next year. They all went to Arnhem the following September. I think Joan wanted to become quite serious in our relationship, but I did not want that and, though I always answered her letters, we never met again.

The Battalion training programme changed again. Each company went off to a different place on detachment, and 'C' Company went to London and stayed in Chelsea Barracks, a depot of the Guards. In the bombed ruins of Battersea across the river was a battle school which was used to learn street fighting. The people had been moved out of an area a mile square, leaving shops, schools and churches as they stood, mostly roofless and damaged from the work of the Luftwaffe.

We learned how to move along a row of terraced houses without entering the street: this was called 'mouseholing'. A wad of gun cotton with a fuse and detonator was placed against each party wall and used to blow a hole through into the next house. Two of us crawled through and dashed from room to room, clearing it of the enemy, who were represented by figure targets. At the same time, a lad would climb over the back walls in the yards, clearing sheds and out-houses. He had the best job: he could breathe; those of us who were in the houses were covered in soot, plaster and filth every time we threw a grenade or blasted through a wall. We used to get under the stairs or in a kitchen till the explosive went off; the dirt was unbelieveable, we were covered from head to foot and looked like Kentucky minstrels. We also ran through and between the houses as figures popped up at doorways and windows. It was good fun and we all enjoyed it.

The lads were always ready for a joke, and we got up to so many tricks that the Guards officers who ran the school never knew whether they were coming or going. I remember one time when the tea-break was in full swing and we were sitting among the rubble, when there was an almighty explosion and dozens of dustbins lifted 30 feet into the air. By the time they landed, everyone had taken cover. Later, two people appeared in the street, one pushing an old pram and dressed in a long black coat, wearing a big hat with ostrich feathers. The other had an old top hat on.

'Who on earth's that?' said the Guards officer, 'Who said they could enter the area?'

When they got closer, we saw they were two of the lads dressed in old clothes found in one of the houses, and when we pulled down the hood of the pram there was a third lad sitting in there with a chamber pot on his head. I don't think the Guards had ever had anyone on their course who had caused so much mischief before.

Back to normal in Bulford again, we got ready for the next big exercise. On various exercises the Glider troops trained alongside us, but they did their airborne training at Netheravon, landing on the airfield in gliders. One day the King and Queen came to see them. It was a wonderful sight to see so many 'planes in the sky and to watch their gliders casting off and coming down all together in such a short time. One glider landed close to Their Majesties, who walked over to see the door open and the jeep and anti-tank gun come riding out at speed, but the door jammed and the troops inside produced some real Airborne language as they struggled to clear it. The Queen (who is now the Queen Mother) is supposed to have said, 'It must be very difficult for them.'

Montgomery also came down to see us, and the whole 6th Airborne was formed up on Salisbury Plain. It took quite some time to get us all in perfect order in straight lines. We stood there for half an hour, and then, when he finally did arrive, he drove into the square we had formed, stood up in his open-top car and said 'Gather round me.' Instead of walking round the ranks as he was supposed to do, he said his piece from the car before driving off again.

We marched into Larkhill, the artillery range close to Stonehenge. We had to line up in extended order and move forward under a creeping barrage of 25-pounder shells of high-explosive live ammunition: it was to give us experience of the sound of shells whistling over our heads and landing only 500 yards in front. The land was soft peat, and wet, so there was no danger unless one fell short, but none ever did. Each gave off a thundering bang and a red ball of fire, followed by black smoke.

The guard room at Bulford was holding five lads who had refused to jump. This was a serious offence, and was automatically punishable by court martial. Security in the guard room was already overstretched, so this resulted in me being detailed to report to Police Corporal McGuinness. A lad from 'B' Company called Dixon, who had very broad shoulders, and Gordon Newton from 'A' company, who like me was over six feet high, had also been given the job of policing. Our new boss was very strict indeed both with his prisoners and with his policemen. Each prisoner was hand-cuffed to his metal bed frame. We all three found the work distasteful.

During the day we were all on duty, but at night there was only one of us remaining to collect passes, which were handed in as people returned from leave. After a week-end we were kept very busy as the trains pulled in to the Bulford sidings, bringing back the boys. Often these trains were so late in arriving that it was well into Monday morning. After 1am we were made to write out the charge sheets for those who were late, and also we had to attend the Company Commander's orders next morning, to give evidence that the accused had returned late. The punishment was seven days' fatigues, and sometimes the culprits would be your own friends in the same company. We just hated the job, but we had to do it or else be put on a charge ourselves.

Food had to be brought in containers from the kitchens a quarter of a mile away for the staff and prisoners. The prisoners were not allowed any cigarettes or other comforts at all. They could take a shower twice a week, and had to be marched one at a time with their hands in cuffs to the wash room; as soon as we got clear of the guard room I used to take off their hand-cuffs and give them each a cigarette and then leave them to shower while I went to have a cup of tea in the NAAFI. Not once did they let me down. I realised that I could have been in serious trouble if they had run off, but I felt very sorry for them. It was not a crime to lose one's nerve, not in my eyes. A court martial was held in every case, although the results were always the same: 84 days in detention (the 'glasshouse').

Once I had to accompany a prisoner to the glasshouse with a sergeant. We had to take him to Yorkshire, and the detention centre was an old mill in Sowerby Bridge near Halifax. We knew what his life would be like. The people on fatigues would have to parade outside the guard room first thing in the morning for inspection by the Corporal, who would then give them work to do for half an hour. Then they had to dash like hell in order to get their own work done before going to breakfast, and if they had no time for a meal before parade, then they had to do without. At dinner time it was the same and at tea time they paraded once more outside the guard room at 6pm in full battle dress with rifle plus equipment. They would then be given five minutes to be back on parade in fatigue order. Work was always available in the kitchens, pan-washing or peeling potatoes, and at 10pm they would be back for inspection on parade in battle dress and full marching service order. It was all designed to make your life very unpleasant. During my whole service I was never charged as a private soldier, and never did any jankers; not that I did not deserve any, I just never got caught.

I decided to see the Company Commander, as things were easing up. There were only two prisoners left in the guard room, so I told him that I did not want to be away from training any longer if I could help it, and a few days later he got me back to 'C' Company.

I had just returned to the Platoon again when a Company detachment was sent to Corfe Castle, near Weymouth and Swanage. The area from the Castle to Poole bay, all the farms and houses and whole small villages, was cleared of civilians completely. We were allowed to use live ammunition without any worries about killing civilians. We lived in a farm house, and used to double down to the sea for a swim, and double back again for breakfast, and then get down to some field practice.

One day I was lying in a field full of turnips where, covered with the big leaves, I could watch a section of road 100 yards away. Suddenly a big hare came up the row of turnips. He stood still for a few seconds right close to my face, then he ran off down another row.

It was the end of March, but quite mild weather. The sun seemed to shine every day in Dorset. A dance was held in the village hall in Corfe, and people turned up from all over the place. I danced with a nurse from Wareham, the next village. I was still struggling to put my feet in the right places; however, she managed to teach me a few steps. Next day I took her to Swanage, where I had a swim, and when I came out of the sea she had brought a tray of cakes and tea from a café near the beach. She was on duty at Wareham Hospital, so we took the train back to Corfe, and that was the last I saw of her, as we moved back to Bulford the next day at short notice.

Very soon we were on the move again, this time to Southampton where, in places, the bombing had been as bad as in London. Close to a factory making Spitfire engines, an area as big as that at Battersea in London had been badly damaged. The enemy seem to have aimed at the factory and missed it, hitting houses just across the river Itchen on the east bank. Inevitably we would get involved in street fighting when we arrived in France, and the CO had ordered some more practice, so this is where we came to spend the next week, going over and over the drills.

Every man in the Battalion was trained to perfection, and the training paid off. We became very good at our job and could deal with any situation. We practised unarmed combat and could break a man's back over one knee in two seconds, or render him totally deaf by ruining his eardrums, or perform other unsavoury actions designed for dealing with sentries quietly.

We always made for the dance halls to meet the girls, and at one dance I met a lovely girl, whose name was Iris. She must have been a year younger than me, and was training to become a hairdresser. From the very first meeting we got on fine and during that week we saw each other two or three times before I left again for Bulford. She said that I could stay at her home on my next weekend leave, and gave me her address not far from the ferry crossing over the Itchen.

I wrote a couple of times before the next week-end passes were issued and, while everyone else dashed off for London, I made my way to Southampton. Her people were very nice, her brother was about my age, and her parents much younger than mine. Bill shared his bed with me and on Sunday Bill, Iris and I went to their chapel, while their mother cooked a lovely dinner to await our return. In the afternoon Iris and I walked along the river Itchen, which flows into Southampton Water where the bigger ships dock. All along the banks were landing-craft, close together, dozens of them, waiting to cross to France when D-Day came. It was very near, but we did not know when it would be. British sailors and Yanks sat about in the sunshine. Iris and I had to say goodbye, but I felt sure that we would have another week-end together before D-Day.

I had to change trains at Winchester for Salisbury. Police were clearing the platform, though they said nothing to me so I remained on the station. Very shortly a special train moved slowly through. There were only three coaches, and sitting in the centre coach was Winston Churchill. He nodded to me as I stood to attention; he knew where I would be in a couple of weeks' time. On the night before D-Day, he said to his wife, Clementine, 'Do you realise that by the time you wake up in the morning, 20,000 men may have been killed?'

Chapter 6

The D-Day Drop –
In the Wrong Place!

Back in Bulford something was happening but we could not find out any details. After every item of kit had been checked and inspected, we marched off along a road ending in a field beside a wood. It was near to Wood Hay, a few miles from Newbury. Here we made our bivouacs along the hedge of hawthorns.

At one corner of the field a large marquee had been erected and, when we had all settled in, it was here that the CO told us why we had come to this area.

'Our final training for D-Day starts here. What I am about to tell you is top secret and not one of you will disclose this information. We have been given an important task for D-Day. On the French coast, the Germans have build a large gun battery, and all attempts to bomb it have failed. One of the beaches close to the guns will be used by the sea-borne forces and unless those guns are put out of action they could blow the landing-craft out of the water before they have the chance to reach the shore.'

We learned all the details, except where in France, or on which day, we would go to destroy the guns; but it was the middle of May, and we expected it would be only a matter of days.

Royal Engineers came with bulldozers and scaffolding, and we helped them to build four large gun emplacements, shaped just like the real thing, but made of framework covered with hessian to represent concrete. A trench four yards deep and four yards wide was scooped out of the ground by mechanical digger, then filled with mines and barbed wire. This represented the anti-tank ditch which ran along the front of the battery site. Miles of wire were pulled out in coils and stretched round the whole area, with more mines, and machine-gun posts marked out to continue the realistic appearance. When all the work on the site was completed, we made plans to attack it.

At first we simply walked into the attack, to make sure of our movements; then we made it as close to the real thing as we could without firing a shot. By this time every one knew just where he was supposed to go, where the enemy troops would be and which ones each of us were detailed to kill. The only things we did not know were their names and the colour of their hair.

All live ammunition would be used from now on. The first full-scale attack was mounted in daylight. At night we did it again, and again the following day and night, the same drill, until we were perfect in every way. Everyone had a special job to do and could do it backwards. The noise of explosions, the machine-gun fire, the flares and the flashes must have kept the villagers awake for the whole week that we were there.

No-one was allowed to enter the area we had trained in, or to know what was going on. The CO reminded us again of the importance of secrecy, before going on to say that we would be allowed a 48-hour pass.

On Saturday morning I went to the public baths in Newbury to get myself cleaned up before going on to Southampton. After living in a bivouac under a hedge all week, I certainly needed it! On my arrival, the attendant said that the place was closed as they did not have any hot water, but after we had chatted he opened the door and let me in: a cold bath was better than none at all.

Iris was still at work when I arrived, but I had a meal with her mother, who had to go into town shopping. I went with her. She was a nice woman, but very fussy, and I hated the way she introduced me to all her friends, telling them that I was Iris's boy-friend. I would have liked to have run a mile, but I was carrying all her parcels!

Everyone could tell that D-Day was almost upon us. In this area of England there was so much equipment, piled up high in fields beside the roads; there were lines of trucks and jeeps, and troops under canvas waiting to step into the landing-craft to sail for France. I was often asked what I had recently been doing, but I kept my mouth shut and managed to skip over the subject.

The week-end passed so quickly and, before I knew what had happened, it was Sunday afternoon. The photographs we had taken in Southampton would not be ready for a week, and I knew it would be unlikely that I would get another leave to collect them. We had tea in a café and I could feel all eyes on us; we were so young, and the maroon beret always attracted

My parents 1941

My second day in the Army, with the Gordon Highlanders, Brig O'Don,
Aberdeen, August 1942

Middlesbrough Station, August 1942, the day after I left for Aberdeen

Airborne forces on parade at Ringway

Soldiers were taught to jump correctly through a hole cut in a high platform to simulate the exit from a Whitley aircraft

9th Parachute Battalion marching in London, 1944

C Company 9th Para, October 1943

This stone stands close to our wartime positions at Chateau St. Come

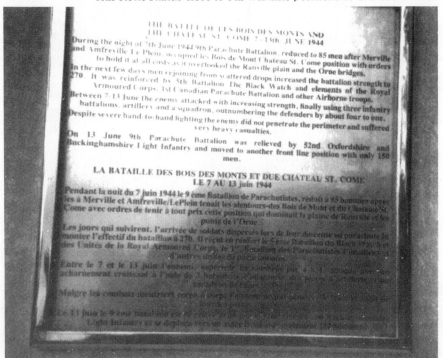

THE BATTLE OF LES BOIS DES MONTS AND
THE CHATEAU ST. COME 7 - 13th JUNE 1944

During the night of 7th June 1944 9th Parachute Battalion, reduced to 85 men after Merville and Amfreville Le Plein, occupied les Bois de Mont Chateau St. Come position with orders to hold it at all costs as it overlooked the Ranville plain and the Orne bridges.

In the next few days men rejoining from scattered drops increased the battalion strength to 270. It was reinforced by 5th Battalion The Black Watch and elements of the Royal Armoured Corps, 1st Canadian Parachute Battalion and other Airborne troops.

Between 7-13 June the enemy attacked with increasing strength, finally using three infantry battalions, artillery and a squadron, outnumbering the defenders by about four to one. Despite severe hand-to-hand fighting the enemy did not penetrate the perimeter and suffered very heavy casualties.

On 13 June 9th Parachute Battalion was relieved by 52nd Oxfordshire and Buckinghamshire Light Infantry and moved to another front line position with only 180 men.

LA BATAILLE DES BOIS DES MONTS ET DUE CHATEAU ST. COME
LE 7 AU 13 juin 1944

Pendant la nuit du 7 juin 1944 le 9 eme Bataillon de Parachutistes, réduit à 85 hommes après les à Merville et Amfreville/LePlein tenait les alentours des Bois de Mont et du Chateau St. Come avec ordres de tenir à tout prix cette position qui dominait la plaine de Ranville et les ponts de l'Orne.

Les jours qui suivirent, l'arrivée de soldats dispersés lors de leur descente en parachute fit monter l'effectif du bataillon à 270. Il reçut en renfort le 5eme Bataillon du Black Watch et des Unités de la Royal Armoured Corps, le 1er Bataillon des Parachutistes Canadiens et d'autres unités aeroportées.

Entre le 7 et le 13 juin l'ennemi, supérieur en combats, par 4 à 1, attaqua avec un acharnement croissant à l'aide de 3 bataillons d'infanterie, avec pièces d'artillerie et un bataillon de chars.

Malgre les combats meurtriers corps à corps l'ennemi n'eut pas...

Le 13 juin le 9 eme bataillon fut releve par le 52eme Oxfordshire et Buckinghamshire Light Infantry et se deploya vers un autre front en n'ayant plus que 180 hommes.

Hatenboer farm on the Maas, Holland

Abbaye de Maredsous

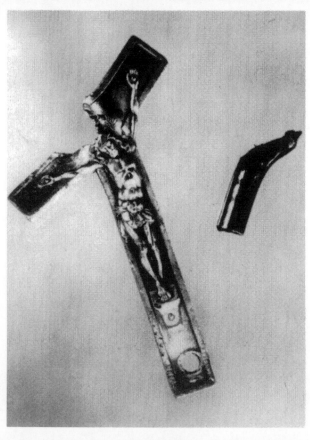

MG42 bullet and the crucifix that saved my life. The hole at the bottom was drilled to fix dog tags

Dorothy and me, June 1945

Our wedding,
Boxing Day 1946

Telephone: Newcastle 24091.

THE GRAND HOTEL,

NEWCASTLE-UPON-TYNE, 2.

CHARGES INCLUDE ENTIRE SERVICE.

No Cheques taken in payment of Hotel Accounts.

M. & Mrs Tucker.   Room 3

NOTE.—ALL ACCOUNTS ARE TO BE SETTLED WEEKLY.

1926

Andrew Reid & Company, Limited. 2219r

	Dec.	26	27	28		
Brought forward						
Apartments and Board		15 -	1 15	3 - -		
Apartments			1 15 -			
Attendance						
Baths						
Fires and Lights....						
Breakfasts						
Luncheons						
Dinners		10.				
Corkage						
Biscuits and Sandwiches						
Teas and Coffee						
Soups						
Suppers						
Servants' Board ...						
Sherry						
Champagnes						
Claret						
Port						
Moselle						
Hock						
Burgundy....						
Madeira						
Chablis and Sauterne						
Brandy						
Whisky						
Gin and Hollands						
Rum						
Liqueurs						
Ale, Stout, etc.						
Aerated Waters						
Cigars						
Sundries						
Stationery						
Washing						
PAID OUT						
Carried forward		1 15	3			

P.S.—Visitors having any complaints to make are requested to communicate at once with the Manageress.

The hotel bill for our wedding night

attention once I was away from Bulford and Salisbury. It never occurred to me that I might not have very long to live, but I imagine older people were thinking on those lines, knowing that the Para were going to France any day. Our goodbyes at the station were to be our last, though of course I had no idea of that at the time. She was the only girl I had thought much about since Dorothy had said goodbye two years before.

Two days after returning to camp we were on the move again, this time to Broadwell Camp. It was comletely sealed off: we could not get out and no-one was allowed in. Here we were told of our destination. It was the Merville battery in Normandy, three miles or so from Sword beach, where the Commandos would land at about 7am. We would drop at a few minutes past midnight, and the guns had to be put out of action by dawn, which would be at 05.00 hours.

We studied the maps and photographs supplied by the RAF. Ammunition was opened, and we could take as much as we wanted. We all had to carry plastic explosive and an anti-tank mine, but we could please ourselves as to how many hand grenades or rounds of ammo we took. We polished and oiled the working parts of our equipment, loading the magazines as carefully as a watch-maker.

General Gale came round to see each battalion. He told us we would be going to a heavily defended area, with 350,000 Panzer, SS and Hitler youth. There were floods and mines, sticks with spikes stuck in the ground. 'In fact', he said, 'it is the last place they would expect us to land and that is why we are going.' Everyone cheered, what the hell for I don't know, but his blunt approach left no-one in doubt that we had our hands full, and perhaps it put us in the right frame of mind. We all knew that the Germans certainly would not be waiting to shake our hands on arrival, and that our jobs had to be completed at all cost.

On Broadwell perimeter Dakotas were lined up, each with a number and all with large black and white stripes painted under their wings and round the fuselage. We fitted 'chutes and chalked our names on them, and they were then placed on the seats on the plane. I was going to jump No. 13, and with a number like that it was considered I would be the first to get shot. This was typical Airborne humour, which was never taken to heart, and to which I replied that I would be the first to have a date with an angel while they silly mugs were fighting for their lives. Later that day we returned to the 'planes, fitted 'chutes, and were waiting to take off, when the word came that the operation was cancelled due to bad weather conditions.

Next day we passed time refilling magazines and cleaning weapons once more. Then we had to don gas-masks and walk through a hut filled with tear gas. Just as we were coming out we had to take them off, to prove that they had been working up till then. It almost choked us. Some of the lads had their hair cut in a Mohican Indian style; we were all cropped very short, to last until we could find time to see to it again.

Our Chaplain, John Guinnett, held a drumhead service and prayed for us all. Everyone respected him deeply. He was one of us, and would jump into Normandy with us, taking the same risks but with only a red cross on his arm and his faith to defend him.

This time, the operation was definitely on, and we were all pleased generally speaking: we knew it had to be done, and the sooner the better. The roar of the 'planes warming up was great, and we took our seats as best we could. With all the equipment it was no easy task. One by one we waited our turn to take off on the runway; then at last it came, the terrific roar as the pilot revved up before taking the brakes off. What a load to lift into the air! but soon we were on our way.

It took almost an hour to form up in the air, and then the 'planes made for the coast. Passing over Southampton, I wondered if Iris knew we were overhead on our way to France. She and her family would be just going to bed at this time, as it was 11pm. The flight across the Channel was smooth and seemed uneventful, although, unknown to us, some gliders full of stores had come down when their tow ropes had snapped.

The coast of France came in sight, but all we could see was thin white lines where the breakers came ashore. Then we passed over them and the whole peaceful scene changed. Streams of red ack-ack came in up long curves. The pilot was swinging the 'plane from side to side, making it very difficult for us to stand up in all our heavy gear.

The green light came on: out we went as fast as we could. I was glad to get out. My 'chute opened, and I could see lots of red flashes from the guns. There seemed to be plenty of those, from where I was looking down at 600 feet. There was lots of water too, which should not have been there. 'Where have they dropped us?' I thought. Just as I was thinking this would be a water jump, a narrow country road appeared beneath me.

Once on dry ground, I was out of my 'chute in seconds, and

this is where I heard heavy footsteps running toward me. After they had run away as quickly as they had come, I removed my rifle from its protective sleeve and made off down the road, keeping to the grass so that I made no noise.

I met Jock Lepper, my Platoon Commander, and with him were Gus Gower and three more lads. Shortly afterwards we met our Company Commander, Major Dyer and continued down the road towards the south-west. Suddenly there were German voices, and before we could do anything they moved quickly past us on cycles, 20 or 30 riding in pairs. We could have touched them, but they must have taken us for their own troops. One of them shouted to Jock and he immediately responded with some similar noise, which they must have accepted, as they just cycled on.

A few moments later, as planes passed over, an 88mm gun opened up; the whole area was lit by its flash and it was as light as day. We saw a platoon of enemy gunners in the field across the road. They must have seen us at the same time. We decided to run along the hedge at 90° to them and the road. Within two minues a machine-gun opened fire. I dived straight into a bed of nettles and the red tracer bullets missed me, whizzing overhead. Everyone seemed to be still intact, and shortly after we moved on again in the same direction. The gun opened fire, and this time they got the lad in the rear; he was hit in the leg, but was able to limp along.

An hour later we came across more Germans in a farmhouse. We were upon them before they could do anything, so Major Dyer threw a hand-grenade at them and we made off again. It was still quite dark, but we could hear gunfire, and explosions every few seconds. Crossing the field we could hear another noise, getting louder and louder. We stood still as it approached, and realised it was the sound of horses' hooves; they were stampeding in panic at all the noise, and had passed by very close indeed. It was a tense few seconds for us all. It was now 2am, and we realised that we had been dropped miles from where we were supposed to have been. A Major and a Colonel appeared, General Gale's General Staff Officers One and Two. They too were miles out of their way.

Already it was getting lighter, and to avoid detection we moved down into the ditches along the sides of the roads. Some of these had three feet of water in them, making for heavy going and slow progress, but we were completely covered. Quite suddenly we came to a clearing between high trees. A hundred yards across a meadow was a house with a six-foot high wall around it. A lad called Berry and I were told to clear it while the rest gave us covering fire. It was now 04.00 hours and quite light. As we ran across the open ground there was no answering fire, which seemed a good start. In seconds we climbed the wall and dashed to each side of the door: still nothing moved. We grabbed the handle and rushed in; remembering the drill of house-clearing we ran from room to room. One room had a dressing table with all kinds of perfume on it, and I stayed long enough to spray some of it around before reporting that all was well to the rest of the party. Downstairs a table was laid, and the flowers in the bowl looked fresh. The others crossed the wall into the house, and we went out on the other side into a road.

We were less than half a mile from a brick works, where there 3rd Brigade planned to establish an HQ. Before reaching it we joined some Canadian Para, who were sitting in a ditch at a cross roads, while the Major and the Colonel went into HQ in the brick yard. This seemed a good opportunity to drop my pants behind a few bushes. No sooner had I done this, than a Junkers bomber came over. I could see the bomb aimer clearly in the perspex nose, which was at tree-top height, and also the pilot's head, looking down. I found I no longer had the need, and quickly pulled up my pants and grabbed my rifle.

An hour later a truck came up the road from Cabourg with six German soldiers in it. We opened fire when it was 50 yards away. It ran off the road into a ditch, and we crawled along the ditch to make sure they were all dead, and just as we reached them, one pulled a pistol from under his coat. It was an Italian 'Beretta' - he must have served in Italy. I shot him at close range, and when we turned him over he had a hole in his back as big as a fist. The truck, which was one that had been captured at Dunkirk, was recovered, and we sent it down to the brick works.

A wire was slung across the road a yard high between two trees and we dug some firing positions facing the open field. A short time later a motor cycle came down the road. The cyclist hit the wire at the same time as he got a bullet in his head, and the BMW was taken down to HQ.

Major Dyer asked me to go down to HQ with him as a bodyguard. I took him along the ditch beside the road and, reaching the entrance to the brick works I saw a large white bulldog with a collar on it, standing beside a kennel. It was so real-looking that it had me fooled, until I noticed there were dozens of little pottery animals in the garden beside the gates. It seems that they were made at the brick works.

While waiting for the Major, I noticed our transport Sergeant struggling to start the BMW with the kick starter. 'Why don't you use the self-starter button?' I asked. He looked at me in amazement. 'It's under the saddle', I said. As soon as he touched it, the engine sprang to life. This was the only time I was able to use the knowledge gained at the Finchley course!

The people living at a farm house close to the brick works came out and brought a bottle of Calvados; they gave me a glass before I went back to the cross roads. An hour later about 200 Germans came out of a wood. They began walking towards our positions alongside the hedge. In all, there were only about 20 of us. I shared a trench with a lad from the 8th Parachute Battalion. The enemy had no idea that we were there, so we let them come within 30 yards before we all opened up. I think a lot of them fell, but quite a number of them crawled back into the woods.

I had never heard bullets whistling past my ears before, but now they were coming through the high grass thick and fast. A Spandau machine-gun was cutting its way through our positions. I had heard that they fired 1,200 rounds a minute, and went through a target like a knife.

I dropped down to re-load my rifle under cover and a second later my friend from the 8th slumped down beside me. There was blood flowing from a neck wound: the Spandau had got him and almost cut his head off. Instinctively I pulled out my shell dressing and covered the wound, but it soaked straight through, covering me with warm blood. I could feel it on my skin. The left leg of my trousers was soaked through with blood. Medics came some time later and pulled him out of the trench and took him to a first aid post. I never heard anything of what had happened to him, but I think he must surely have died.

The enemy were appearing all along the side of the road, making for the house we had occupied that morning; they were only 100 yards away. Jock Lepper was ordered to take the house before the Germans did, and he took Gus Gower, Private Fenton, a Bren gunner, and me. We made a dash for it, and I could feel the draught from the German bullets as they flew past our heads. Reaching the house, we closed the two large green doors behind us, and felt much safer: there was a high, stout wall at the back.

When we took up positions by the windows, we saw the

Germans were in a ditch across the road, firing into the rooms at point blank range. They came across to fire stick grenades into the downstairs rooms, bringing plaster and dust down on top of us as we hid behind the furniture. Jock thought that the Bren gunner might be able to clear a few of them if he got into the ditch outside, and sent him out to try, but he was shot immediately he left the house.

The firing went on all afternoon and all night non-stop, until the house was beginning to fall apart. Next morning I tried to make some tea in one of the small rooms. I was sitting with my back to the wall facing the door, and a shell came through the wall three feet above my head, making a hole half a yard round, and the blast carried me out into the yard and threw me full length 20 yards away. I was shaken but unhurt; the mess tin with the tea in it had disappeared. The shell had not exploded, but must have gone straight through the doorway at the other side of the house and taken me with it. It was non-stop excitement, and we were very worried about the lads at the cross roads who were so heavily outnumbered. We believed that they had been killed by now and that we were the only survivors.

The trouble was that we were running out of ammunition, but firing was now coming at us from all directions and we had no means of escape. The perimeter wall was half a yard thick, and it was safe behind it as long as we kept the enemy from coming through the door and windows; but by 5pm we had come to the final stage. We knew that soon the Germans would rush the large wooden doors into the yard.

Gus and I had dug a position facing the doors, and we waited. We had one '36' grenade between us, and agreed to pull the pin if we were overrun. Half an hour later, and it seemed a long half-hour, the doors burst open, and just as we were about to fire our last rounds we saw Captain Robinson, followed by a few of the lads. He put his arms around Jock Lepper and there were tears in his eyes, for they too had thought we had been wiped out. During the night reinforcements had arrived and held back the German battalion that had caused us so much trouble. As we left we saw both Canadian and German bodies lying about, some only a few feet away from the doorway into the house.

We were all sent back to the brick works and told to dig in before we could have any food. Mortar bombs were causing many of the casualties, so it was important to get a hole dug if you wanted to stay alive. Meanwhile we heard about the few lads of the 9th Battalion who had managed to get to the Rendezvous in time. They attacked the Merville Battery and did the job; but of the 150 lads who had attacked and captured the battery, only 75 were left standing.

Chapter 7

Bitter Fighting in Normandy – Château St Come

The main part of the 9th Battalion was now dug in on some high ground a mile away at the Château St Come. My trench at the brick works was almost finished when an urgent message was received: all members of the 9th had to report to the Château. So we did not get anything to eat after all, (though I managed to fill my water bottle).

Instead, we moved along a wooded lane leading to the Château. Suddenly shells started bursting among the trees. This was our first experience of shell fire without any cover, and what made it worse was that they were our own shells, which the glider boys had brought down with them! Wireless messages were received, with apologies. It was dark now, well after 10pm, and we moved on. I had taken over the Bren gun from the lad who was shot at the farmhouse. When we reached the remnants of the 9th, which had been taking some punishment, the CO said, 'Where the hell have you been?' and ordered us out on a fighting patrol.

At midnight we moved out to the Geman positions. Reaching the edge of the wood, we came across a box of twelve full magazines suitable for the Bren, so Major Dyer, our Company Commander, told me to use them to fire into what he thought was the enemy positions. Firing the 336 rounds, I covered the area as though I was watering the garden with a hose pipe. The gun barrel was so hot that I could feel it burning my hands as I carried it on for our next move, which was into the Château gardens. The Château itself was empty, and we lay down in a large circle between two rows of trees, at least twenty of us. We were very close to the Germans, but could not detect their exact positions. After about twenty minutes the word came for us to take up new positions 200 yards away.

It was pitch black. I lay down next to Reg Fowler, the Corporal in charge of me and the Bren. We were all extremely tired and hungry, and the time seemed to drag. Just then a mortar bomb stonk came down (stonk was the name given to a shower of bombs), and landed in the position we had just left. This lasted ten minutes, then all was quiet again. An hour later, word came to move on once more. I thumped Reg Fowler, thinking he was asleep, but he did not move, so I gave him a really hard dig with my elbow. Still there was no movement. I put my hand on his face: it was ice cold.

I had been laid down next to a dead German, and Reg was looking for me!

There had been some trouble from stables at the rear of the Château, and I was sent for. Jock Lepper told me to put a burst of Bren fire in at each of the windows and the doorway. The straw inside caught fire, but no-one came out. Going further on, at dawn, we found the bodies of Sergeant Rose and Ginger Parfitt, his Platoon Commander. Sergeant Rose had been the victim of a Spandau: the top of his head had been cut clean off in an attack in this area on the previous day. We brought the bodies back into our wooded area at the bottom of the Château drive.

It was now daylight, and looking at the lads who were left from the 9th Battalion brought a lump to my throat. Out of the 600 dropped there were hardly 100 of us left; still, more could turn up as the days went by.

At long last we dug in and had a much needed meal, our first for three days, and we were able to enjoy three hours' sleep before the shelling started. German air-burst shells had leaflets in them, telling us about the new weapon which 'is devastating London at this very moment. Soon to be directed at every town and city in the UK'. This was the flying bomb. Another leaflet told us about the Yanks taking our wives and girlfriends, and had a picture of a bedroom scene. It asked us to lay down our arms and save our loved ones at home.

We sent out patrols at night in the hopes of snatching an unsuspecting soldier and bringing him back for questioning. The Germans did the same, and would pass close by us. It was important to keep our whereabouts secret, and not to fire a weapon during the hours of darkness. A soldier whom we brought in one night was found to be Russian, and told us everything about his unit, its strength, armour etc. The German NCO's had told him that our Paratroops did not take prisoners. Similarly, their own troops had been told not to spare us, as can be seen in these instructions found on a German Army notice board in a Headquarters in Normandy:

German Supreme Command, Berlin, for Wehrmacht Publication Report. (Hitler)

I command from now on, German troops will destroy to the last man all enemy troops taking part in so-called Commando raids in Europe, whether it is a case of soldiers in uniform, or of sabotage troops, with or without weapons, whether in battle or whilst escaping. It is immaterial whether they are brought into action by sea or parachute. Even should these creatures, when captured, show readiness to surrender, they are on no account to be shown the slightest mercy.

The ground we held was the highest point in the area. Here the Germans could have sited their guns and destroyed the bridge over the Orne river and canal, and done untold damage to the sea-borne troops and to the supplies, which would be desperately needed if we were to hold out against the German infantry and the Panzer divisions which were trying to get to the coast. Our troops were coming ashore every day, but similarly the enemy were bringing up troops between us and the coast, from the Cabourg area.

Each time they attacked our positions they were more determined, and they were fresh troops too. Also they had more support, as they brought up heavy artillery and a large mortar which we called 'Moaning Minnie'. Sometimes the bombs were full of phosphorus, which stuck to the trees and burned for hours, giving off a sickly, acrid-smelling smoke. If any of it touched clothing, the garment had to be taken off immediately before the phosphorus burned the skin. The tops of the trees came crashing down, cut by the shell splinters, and the branches which fell around our slit trenches helped to conceal our positions.

We were well dug into our trenches in thick undergrowth, and the Germans did not know where until it was too late. We killed them all at very close range, so as not to miss, but they still came, till there were so many dead bodies that there was a horrible putrid smell. The bodies started to swell up and were covered with bluebottles and other flies, which came over in a black cloud to descend on them.

The artillery would pound us for hours before they sent in the infantry to finish us off, but we hardly had a single casualty from shelling. We just sat in the bottom of the trench, singing:

Oh dear, what can the matter be?
Three old maids got locked in a lavatory,
They were there from Monday to Saturday
And nobody knew they were there.

As soon as the shelling stopped we were waiting for them, ready for the infantry coming blindly on to our sights.

After four days they were backed up with tanks, and things became really serious. We were sent three British Sherman tanks to help out. They pulled into the Château drive one after the other. Suddenly the first one lost its gun turret, blown clean off; the other two 'brewed up', as we called it, set on fire by the enemy 88s. We only had one heavy machine-gun, ~~and~~ a Vickers, which Sergeant McGeever and Corporal McGuinness, the policeman, used like true professionals. Mounted on our only jeep, they ran up and down the road, cutting the Germans down like corn. They changed their postion so frequently that the enemy must have thought there were several Vickers's.

One afternoon a new company of Germans arrived and took up positions alongside a wood in full view of our trenches. We waited until they had got settled to digging in, then all the machine-guns we had opened up, and we wiped out every one of them.

Every time a shell bursts, it gives off cordite fumes that seem to hang heavily at ground level, combined with the smell of dead bodies and phosphorus. The cocktail of odours is so revolting that you feel permanently sick.

We began to have a lot of casualties from mortar bombs and we were getting thin on the ground. Our nearest troops were two miles away at the brick works; down the hill from them the 7th and 13th Battalions were heavily engaged at Ranville village and the bridge over the Orne river and canal. The Glider troops had their anti-tank six-pounder guns in position, wating for the full might of the Panzers, between Ranville and the waterways.

However, General Gale was allowed a battalion of Black Watch to help out, and he sent them to the Château St Come. We watched as they came across a field, and we could not believe our eyes. They walked across as if they were in England, not in a battle area! As expected, the Boche opened up with machine gun and mortar fire, killing and wounding half the Battalion. The rest ran for their lives right into our position, in complete confusion. Our Colonel got them into an organised company and sent them to occupy the Château. The ten Bren gun carriers which the Black Watch used were all knocked out one after the other by the German self-propelled guns and tanks. At this critical stage of the battle John Gwinnett, our padre, nailed the Battalion flag to a tree.

A bungalow in the wooded area of our positions was used as a first aid post and the Battalion HQ. Our MO, Captain Harold Watts, worked continuously during the six days of battle around St Come and at one time had 180 wounded in the medical aid post. On the premises were a Fenchman and his Dutch wife, who were eventually escorted during the night to Ranville for their own safety, much distressed. John Gwinnett worked very hard with the Medics to collect the wounded and also the bodies of the Black Watch, which were laid in the back garden of the bungalow, so close that they were almost piled up. The Dutch woman said to the Padre, 'Are you a Catholic priest?'

'No,' said John, 'Church of England.'

She then said, 'I thought so, you would have had more respect for the dead if you had been Catholic.'

John replied, 'I'm sorry, Madam, but my concern is for the lads still living, who are fighting for their lives.'

My slit trench was 30 yards from the aid post, where amputations and soiled dressings were piled up outside. The ground had a slight incline. One night it had rained heavily and at first light I noticed a stream of watery blood running down the slope and into the trench. I quickly built a wall of clay to prevent it. The whole area we were defending was no more than two acres in extent.

No-one had any sleep for more than two or three hours at a time during those six days of continual attacks. To say that these were ferocious is an understatement. We were short of food and ammunition and needed reinforcements. The RSM, Bill Cunningham, took our jeep and made two daring trips along the mile of road to the brick works, to bring our much needed supplies.

We had but one mortar, which was manned by Sergeant Hennesey and by Gus Gower, who had been made a corporal. It had to be fired in an almost vertical position, as the bombs were required to fall so close to our front. HMS *Arethusa*'s guns were at our disposal, and a radio link brought their fire down to within 500 yards of our own positions; yet they had the nerve (so it was said) to ask us not to request fire during meal times, as the vibration of the guns upset their soup and coffee!

We did not take many prisoners, as we had no-one spare to

look after them, but a few wounded Germans were brought into our aid post, including a major who told Colonel Otway that we had killed or wounded his whole battalion. Otway then told him that we had never been more than 270 strong until the arrival of the Black Watch.

Finally, on the sixth day, General Gale ordered the 12th Battalion to come to our aid and, after a barrage lasting three hours, they captured Breville and cleaned up the German positions completely. The 12th Battalion had lost a lot of lads in the attack, including my friend Norman Parr. We found that a Battalion of Ox and Bucks Glider troops also had come to relieve us.

It was the 13th June, and since landing on the 6th we had only snatched an hour or sometimes three hours' sleep when we could, and food had been mainly hard biscuits and dark, rich chocolate. With our weapons carried at the waist with bayonets permanently fixed, we left the Château in single file, moving down a sunken ditch. I must have been walking while asleep, since my bayonet pricked the bottom of the lad walking in front of me when we halted!

We moved back into the brick works area of Le Mesnil for a rest. It was still a front line position but the enemy in this area were only sending a few mortar bombs and the odd shell over. The medics came round: each lad was de-loused with DDT powder, a long probe being pushed up each sleeve and the powder puffed into the armpits, and again down the front of the trousers, and again down the back of the neck.

There was little rest for me, however. I was sent to fill sand bags with earth, to help build a command post centre for the Brigadier. Afterwards I managed to get four hours' sleep, then was detailed for standing patrol. This consisted of a corporal and two privates, including myself. We had to take the Bren gun and crawl along a ditch toward the German positions, so that we were, in fact, half way between our lines and theirs. The idea was for us to provide an alarm signal, since, should they decide to attack, they would meet us first! We were to move out at dusk and return at first light.

To get to the half-way mark involved crawling 60 yards and over three dead Germans. They had been there a few days and were stinking to high heaven and swelling up horribly. It was nerve-wracking, lying there motionless at the bottom of a wet ditch, waiting to see if the enemy would crawl along from the other end. The ditch was not straight, so we could only see a few feet, and in any case it was full of undergrowth. It seemed particularly ironic that at the other end of this ditch the Germans were now occuping the house that Gus, Jock and I had held a week earlier.

As soon as the bluebottles had stopped their activity for the day, squadrons of mosquitos took over the air space and pounded away at any exposed skin; the backs of our hands, our faces and eyelids were bitten mercilessly. What made it worse was that we dared not move to knock them off and had to suffer the stings continually. The relief that came when we could move out was heaven! I was allowed to sleep from 5am to 8am, then filled sand bags till 4pm, had a meal, and slept till 8.30, before going on 'standing patrol' again.

By this time I was suffering from fatigue. Boils appeared on my neck under the chin, close together, and made it difficult to move my head from side to side. During the night I committed the worst sin imaginable: I fell asleep at my post. It was not intended, but I could not help myself, feeling so weak. The Corporal placed me on a charge when we arrived back in the lines, but the Company Commander, Ian Dyer, never said a word except to tell me to report to the MO.

Doctor Marquis was established at the brigade HQ, in an old farm cottage, and had done some wonderful work here since D-Day. At one stage, with all his instruments lost in the swamps, he had operated and saved lives using razor blades. Now his instruments had been replaced, but he took a strip of wallpaper which was hanging off the walls, and I was told to hold it under my chin while he lanced the boils. Down came a horrible sticky mess, making me feel sick. At that moment one of the lads was brought in with a chunk of mortar bomb stuck in his shoulder. Doctor Marquis dug it out, gave him a transfusion, and then left the Corporal Medic to see to him while he wrote out a form for me to go for a rest down at the beaches.

A jeep picked me up a few minutes later and off we went, down toward the canal bridge (Pegasus Bridge) which had been the very first target for attack by our Division a week earlier, then on toward the beaches about four miles away. The activity down there was furious: men and materials were rushing ashore from landing-craft. Along the coast we came to an area surrounded by a wall very like the one at the farmhouse I had been in shortly after landing. Inside was a tented area. The first tent had showers set up and, stripping off, I was told to keep my boots and smock and leave all the rest behind.

It was simply glorious to feel clean again, especially since my pants had been black with bloodstains. Moving along, I was given new clothing, all the lot, even socks and a towel. There were no regulations: I could go to bed in a tent which was dug out to a depth of three feet and lined with straw, and get up when I felt like it. There was always a meal ready in the biggest of the tents if I wanted to eat. I joined two other lads already asleep in the next tent I opened. I just collapsed on the straw, pulled a blanket over me, and was out like a light for the next eighteen hours. I got up for a meal and then went back to bed, and eight hours later I woke up at 6pm and visited the food tent again. There were newspapers to read, and I listened to the radio. It was so peaceful; I felt much better, and the clean clothes were wonderful. The noise of the traffic was music compared with the sound of shells and mortars. I was able to relax without watching for snipers in the trees, or listening for the 'plop', the tell-tale noise of mortar bombs on their way.

St Aubin-Sur-Mer was only a small seaside town, but now it was a hive of activity, with transport parked and stores piled up, ready to move to the battle front. I could not help but notice the condition in which the troops, Royal Army Service Corps and Pioneers, were working compared to life at the front twelve miles away. We had not tasted fresh bread yet, but lived on hard biscuits, and very hard they were too. These chaps were sitting outside cafés talking to the locals, though we had seen very few of these since D-Day; where they went I have no idea. I knew that there were sixteen men behind the lines to every one man up at the sharp end, and of course we could not do our work without them. The lads running this little holiday camp were worth their weight in gold as far as I was concerned. A cinema show was put on in an old barn on my last day, so I watched the film and was in bed at 10pm. Tomorrow I would be back at the sharp end.

I was up at 8am feeling like a new man, and ate a grand breakfast with two eggs, bacon and lovely new bread. When you have been without bread for a couple of weeks, it tastes like cake. I just had time to write a letter home, the first for some time, before the jeep came to take me back. I began to wonder if the charge of falling asleep would now have to be answered, and what the punishment would be. When I reported to the Company Commander, he smiled and seemed pleased to see me back. I was looking much cleaner than anyone else, in my new shirt and trousers.

'You are improperly dressed', said Major Dyer. 'You should be wearing a stripe, Corporal.'

Chapter 8

Bois de Bavent, Caen Falls, the Boche Retreat

Jock told me I had been promoted, and the promotion was back-dated to D-Day, which meant I would be paid extra money from that day. He also mentioned that he had recommended both Gus and myself for the Military Medal, but that there had been so many great deeds done, and there were only eight MM's allocated to the Battalion, so the promotion of Gus and me was by way of a compromise. We all thought that Jock should have been awarded at least a Military Cross.

The RSM had been killed by an 88mm shell while I had been away. He had been very well liked and respected, and would be missed badly. The Battalion had been moved to the River Orne banks, out of range of the enemy's small arms and mortars, but we could still be shelled by the heavy guns. On one or two nights the Luftwaffe came over to bomb the bridges, but that was comparatively tame after our experiences in the Château, and did not bother us.

My own life became considerably easier: instead of continually jumping into action when orders were dished out, I found that indeed it was my job to give orders, and to supervise their completion. New recruits were arriving from the beach-head, a mixture of Fusiliers and other regiments. Until Para replacements could be sent, the newcomers would be attached to the 9th Para, for our role was still that of an infantry battalion for some weeks to come. They were all at least three years older than me, and I could feel their resentment at being in a section with a young NCO.

When they were lined up one morning soon after they arrived, the guns in the next field opened fire. They were 25-pounders and made a terrific bang. The new chaps lay flat immediately; it had given them a shock. They were surprised to see me still standing. It gave me great pleasure to assure them that these were our own guns, and tell them to drop down to the ground only if they saw me do so; after a few days they would be able to tell the different noises the guns made, and know whom they belonged to.

Guards were still posted at night, but now all I had to do was to see that they changed over at the right time, and between changing guards I could sleep. What a wonderful improvement in my lifestyle! The next few days were spent with the new members of the battalion, showing them how we did things - and that was at the double and no questions asked: that way we lived longer.

Some of the new lads found our ways acceptable and stayed on to do a course and learn how to jump; others went back to their regiments and were glad to do so. We had had our rest, and now it was up to us to relieve the 8th Battalion, which was in a big wooded area, Bois de Bavent. Taking over their postitions was an easy task, as the trenches were already dug for us to occupy.

A German tank there still had the charred remains of its crew in it, but at least they did not smell too much. An anti-tank gun shell had split the tank's front axle, several inches thick, just as if it had been made of wood. By this time every horse and cow in our part of Normandy was lying on its back with its legs in the air and its body blown up to twice the normal size. The bluebottles and flies never had it so good, and the sight of horrible maggots busily chewing away was horrendous. All signs of bird life had disappeared.

From day one, we placed trip flares around our position: empty bean cans on wire between the bushes. They would give good warning of any intruders during the hours of darkness. Apart from the mortaring, we found it a quiet area. Perhaps the rain had a lot to do with it: it came down for four days, making life pretty miserable. Patrols were sent out to make sure that the Boche were not planning to do anything suddenly. They had been continually bashed, and I believe that they were content to sit tight and hope that their Panzers would get through.

But the Panzers were all heavily engaged around the west side of Caen. The Canadians were keeping them busy, and more support was reaching the beaches every day. A Bren carrier came up to us with a supply of ammunition, including mortar bombs; it was just an unlucky hit, but a mortar bomb dropped right into it, exploding and burning everything. We had to sit in our trenches for three hours before the bombs and ammo had finished flying in all directions.

81

Later a further attack of mortars caught Reg Fowler, He died quickly. I was very fond of the Blackpool lad. After our last leave he had returned looking very unhappy, for some personal reasons. We were sorry that his last weeks had been clouded by difficulties at home. On D-Day he had been a corporal, but owing to the heavy casualties, promotions had been frequent, and he had been made sergeant a few days before his death.

The same mortar also wounded another mate of mine, Sid Capon. George Bosher managed to give Sid a drink of tea before the medics took him away. This was typical of George; he was a wonderful mate to have.

While I had been working in the guard room back in Bulford camp as a policeman, Corporal Mc Guiness made me place Sid on a charge sheet 252 for being late returning from leave. He received seven days Confined to Barracks, and I don't think he ever really forgave me.

Sid had been one of the members of 'C' Company who had reached the Rendezvous on D-Day and attacked the Merville guns, along with Johnnie Walker from Stoke-on-Trent and Frank Delsinore from Crawley. They had charged their way across minefields in a torrent of machine-gun fire, which was criss-crossing the gun site from the Germans' well sited and sandbagged positions and trenches. Reaching No. 1 gun, they dropped '36' grenades down the air vent pipes. They could hear the German soldiers shouting within, and chucked more grenades into the recessed entrance of the large concrete casement. The Germans came out, about twenty in all, throwing their weapons on the ground and putting their hands up in terror. They expected to be shot, and kept repeating, 'Kamerade, kamerade, no shoot, no shoot', having been told that the Paras never take prisoners. Sid said that most of them were covered in blood from their wounds.

At last we saw the sun come out; it had stopped raining, and four Typhoons were diving towards our positions! Just as we were about to give them a wave, they fired their rockets and cannon at us; they might have seen the German tank and our Bren gun carrier smouldering, and mistaken us for Germans. Two days later a message came through with their apologies for the straffing.

Colonel Otway had been sent home. He needed a rest: his nerves were very bad and he was losing his balance. A new Colonel arrived, whose name was Napier Crookenden. Paying his respects to 'C' Company, he was very concerned with the number of casualties we were receiving from mortar bombs. We had noted that the mortaring always stopped at dinner time, from 12 to 1pm.

He called for six NCO's from the Company, and we went deep into the wood looking for the culprits. It was their lunch time and we could hear the scrape of mess tins. They were in a small hollow - 20 to 30 Boche, all eating. Around them was the mobile mortar and also, on fixed lines, three heavy machine-guns. We took the firing pins out of the machine-guns and made careful record of the map reference. When we got back, our mortar boys put down a stonk, and we did not have any more trouble from them.

Ten days after we took over these positions, we moved back down the Orne river again. One morning at about 10am my section was cleaning weapons; our machine-gun was stripped down in pieces on a cloth on top of the trench, when suddenly eight ME 109s came over at 300 feet. They buzzed past in seconds, and I have never seen anyone move as fast as we did. I dived clean into the trench head-first, as if I was at the swimming pool. They went toward the beaches, and did not come back our way.

Stores arrived, and new socks and towels, shirts and trousers were issued in exchange for the grubby clothes we had been wearing since our arrival in France. I was lucky: this was my second exchange of clothing!

Each day, every section of around fourteen men received a box of rations, called A, B, C or D packs. Each had a different menu, so arranged as to give us a varied diet. Each included a tin of hard biscuits, some boiled sweets, chocolate, cigarettes and matches, sheets of toilet paper and a tin of sterilising tablets, to use in water bottles. All the food was in tins: the tea, sugar, milk, stew, bacon, fruit cake, creamed rice and many other delicious foods. In all it was a very good system; we had tins of corned beef, but not every day like they did in 1914.

Each section did its own cooking and, so that we did not make any smoke, we used petrol for heating food. This was done by filling a biscuit tin with soil, which would then burn for an hour or so with as little as a pint of petrol poured over it, completely without smoke.

The kitchens set up near the beaches were now sending us some fresh baked bread, which was a real treat. Since we were last here, a Bailey bridge had been completed over the Orne and all kinds of transport was crossing over. A big push was about to take place. One thousand Lancaster bombers came over in staggered formation at about 2,000 feet, heading for Caen just three miles away. Brigadier James Hill jumped into my trench and asked me if I could see anything moving around Caen.

'No, sir, I can't'

He said, 'Have a look through my field glasses.'

These glasses were the best I had ever used, and through them tanks could easily be seen, moving into the dust rising from the city on the other side of the Orne.

The Germans were so well dug in, they were holding up our advance. The bombers made such a mess of the city; even our ears were ringing with the terrible noise, so it must have been sheer hell to be under that attack. Brown smoke and dust was rising high in the air. While all this was going on, our infantry was firing away too, and then the Canadians went in and finally crushed the 12th Panzer Division.

It was heard that the Germans were wandering about like drunken men, completely shocked by the bombing and shelling. This was on June 26th, but the battle did not finish until July 9th. Then our push continued against the Panzer Lehr Division and the 2nd Panzer Division, towards the Falaise Gap, on 7th-29th August.

We received some mail, and I got two parcels. One was from Iris, with tooth-paste, soap and a flannel, and one was from home. My Mother had taken it to heart when she had read my letter about the hard biscuits and no bread to eat, so there was a home-made loaf and a fruit cake, not too well packed in some brown paper and it was just a mass of crumbs, but it still tasted lovely, though it was a hard job getting it into my mouth without swallowing a horde of flies that descended on the food as it was uncovered. The Wright's coal tar soap smelt so good that I decided to have a wash down with it. I boiled some water in a biscuit tin, stripped off completely, and was showering myself down feeling nice and fresh, when the bloody mortars came over. Instinctively I dived into my trench, and emerged a few seconds later covered in mud, to howls of laughter and hoots of delight from the lads.

Gus Gower and I were sent out with sections to seek the enemy, who were thought to have moved out. We had only gone a few hundred yards when we could smell them - they had a smell of their own. Their trenches must have been left in a hurry, for they could not have been gone long. We sent word of this back with a runner, who returned to say we had to wait and hold their positions, as the Brigade was moving up. All I could think of was my parcel with the cake and bread crumbs, which would have to be left if we were to follow the German withdrawal. Fortunately I had the soap and tooth-paste in my haversack.

An hour later the rest of the Company reached us and we continued on our way along a railway track. We came to a bridge over the river Dives, which our engineers had blown up on the night of D-Day. With the bridge being under some feet of water and lying at an angle, it was awkward to feel a way across in the dark. It was midnight and the water reached my chin as I held my weapon above my head. How the small lads managed to keep their heads above water I don't know. Private Speechly was about 5' 3" (160cm), so Private Bosher, who was 6' 2", lifted him on his shoulders and carried him across; he was so proud of the fact that he was the only man in the Battalion who had stayed dry that night!

On the bank at the other side I bent over to let the water run out of my equipment, then took off my steel helmet to empty it. A mile further on, the railway crossed the main Dozulé road and went into the station, with a high embankment on one side. We could hear the German transport in Dozulé, tracked vehicles moving, half a mile away. It was almost dawn. We spread out along the embankment and started to dig in as fast as we could.

My trench was only a foot deep when the Boche opened fire with deadly 88s. I tried desperately to get three feet underground, pressing my head down as far as I could into the shallow trench. We lost a few lads here, and my friend Johnny Walker had a huge chunk of shrapnel stuck in his back. As soon as the shelling stopped we dug deeper, and worked so fast that the steam was rising from our wet clothes as they dried out from the night before. The shelling started again, but now we were covered and only a direct hit would do any damage. The fox holes were a yard deep.

As soon as the guns stopped firing the German infantry, as we expected, started coming across the field at the other side of the railway line. They stretched across the field in single lines with the NCO's behind them, ready to shoot anyone who dared turn back. We let them come to within 50 yards and then cut them down as we all opened fire together. A few still moved, but they were soon finished off. A Spandau machine gun was firing from the ditch running alongside the road from Dozulé, and it was well covered, so we used a 2-inch mortar with HE (high explosive) bombs, and it went quiet.

The 13th Battalion, who were running at 90° from us along a ridge, had seen the Germans coming across the field towards us, but had also waited until we had opened fire. Apart from a few more shells coming over, it was looking good: the enemy seemed to have had enough of us for one day.

During the night 'Bucket' Laurence, so named because he had a face like a bucket, went out and took about a dozen watches from the dead Germans lying where they had fallen. He had six on each wrist.

One of our sergeants had lost all his family in the bombing raids on the London East End, and Private Thomas from the same area had had some family losses too. They were anxious to kill as many Germans as they could and would volunteer for every patrol and appear on the scene where every German WHERE was thought to be. Thomas carried a fighting knife. As we returned one morning from a night patrol, Thomas was cleaning his knife, which was bloodstained. At some time and against orders, he must have crawled off on his own and found himself another Boche. He was a very quiet lad and had little to say, but we all knew he was pretty ruthless.

The 12th, 13th and 7th Battalions had moved out, to chase the Germans retreating toward the river Risle, where they were expected to make a stand. We made our way through into Dozulé, passing the two German gunners lying in the ditch where the two-inch mortar had caught them. They had only been there a couple of days but already their noses and eyes were full of maggots, a truly sickening sight, even on the enemy.

The Boche had shot civilians left in the village; it was hard to tell how many, as all the buildings were blazing. Some of them were ready to drop as the roof beams burned through, and we had to keep in the centre of the road. The 5th Brigade in front of us must have been moving fast, as we were going at a good pace.

A little further south, the remnants of the 12th Panzer Division were safely out of the Falaise gap and also heading for the Risle at speed. On D-Day, their orders had been to make for the coast along the east bank of the Orne, shortly after passing Caen. Berlin then instructed them to move to the west bank and head for the beaches. Had they come direct into our area on the eastern side, we would have been unable to stop them with our light armament.

Twelve years later, I was given this information by a member of the 12th Panzer. His name was John, and in 1937 the Germans had moved into his country, a quiet farming area of Czechoslovakia close to the Polish border. John was thirteen years old, and saw the Germans shoot his father by firing squad. Along with other young men, he was taken to Germany to work in a steel works for twelve hours a day and be poorly fed in return. At seventeen he was forced to become a soldier, and was in charge of a horse-drawn water cart attached to the 12th Panzer Division.

As the Falaise gap closed, the Boche were trying desperately to escape, with so many of the infantry hanging on to tanks that the German gunners could not identify their own tanks, and fired on them. John saw this happen. He and his Polish friend wanted to be taken prisoner but the Hitler Youth NCO's would have shot them had they shown any sign of surrender. It was several months later, while they were in the cellar of a house during shelling, that the opportunity came. The building came down but they made no attempt to dig themselves out; they waited for three days until they were sure that British troops had taken the area.

Within six weeks John had changed uniform and was fighting the Germans with the Polish Brigade. He was demobilised in Sheffield in 1946 and married a local girl, and I met him while working for the same firm when he was posted to Middlesbrough. We became firm friends; he was a true Christian and I will never forget his kindness. He died in 1978.

The 9th Para waited in the orchard just off the road leading to Pont l'Evéque. It was to be a night attack. Dozulé was several miles behind us now and we pressed on at a good pace, but as expected the Boche intended to make a stand. Close to the river Risle we made a meal from our 48-hour ration packs and there was time for an hour's sleep. We had not had any sleep for two days.

At 10pm the order came to move. Outside on the orchard road, I noticed I was one man short in the section and returned to look for him. Private Wood was still asleep, and I had to give him a rocket for causing the delay. In the dark, dashing back on to the road, I fell into a German trench with a terrific bang.

Chapter 9

Convalescence

My left leg was completely numb and absolutely dead; I could not feel it, so I thought it must be broken. Jock Lepper came looking for me, but I could not move. With some help I managed to get on to the road, and the others left me at the Calvary cross there, saying that they would report me to the Medics, who would pick me up. Leaving me with my rifle, Jock took my automatic; it would be useful to him if street fighting developed in Pont l'Evéque.

About an hour later I thought I could see a small beam of light in the garden of a cottage on the other side of the road. I decided to investigate. It took me half an hour to crawl to the light, dragging my left leg along. The light came from a shelter, which had steps leading down to the doorway, and in the dark I crashed down them, banging my head against the door. The people inside were terrified, and I could hear the children crying. I did my best to assure them that I was British, but it took some time before an old man opened the door an inch. At last they became convinced that I was not German and then they quickly pulled me inside the shelter.

There was noise of battle down the road and these poor people were very frightened. I was given a bunk to lie on while they cut my boot laces and eased the boot off. My ankle was swollen and extremely painful. They gave me a glass of Calvados and then I passed out completely. It must have been about 6am when I woke up to a row of little faces solemnly looking at me. The oldest child had a plate of soup and a piece of bread. They watched while I ate. They must have heard that the Boche were on the move again, going further away from them, as they seemed a lot happier.

Shortly after, an ambulance arrived with the Medics. It was a lovely morning, bright and sunny: August 22nd 1944. The field ambulance men carried me to their vehicle, and the French family all stood round waiting to shake hands. Before moving off, I managed to assure them that the Boche had gone for good; it was great to see all their smiling faces, which needed no words.

An Airborne lieutenant in the Engineers was on the stretcher at the other side of the ambulance, with a shrapnel wound. We travelled for three hours before reaching the Orne bridge (now called Pegasus Bridge). We continued along the coast, and an hour later reached the 73rd Field Hospital at Bayeux. Long tents housed the wards of beds. After an immediate check at reception, I was taken to one of the tents. The lieutenant was creating hell as they carried him off to another ward: he kept insisting that we should be together. I don't know what happened, but I was put in a bed in another ward. I should think he would have been put in a ward for officers.

The Airborne are different from other units in the Army: the officers endure the same conditions as other ranks. The result is a very healthy respect for each other; it does not affect discipline at all but the comradeship is second to none.

On 26th August, along with other wounded, we were taken on a DUKW, a wheeled vehicle shaped like a boat. This took us to Arromanches and drove along the beach and into the sea for a mile, out to the hospital boat. There was a door open almost at sea level in the side. I asked to be put down where I could see what was going on, as supplies were being unloaded and dozens of trucks were being driven along the piers toward the shore. Soon the lines were pulled aboard and we began to move off, leaving all the activity. Arromanches must have been the busiest port in the world at that time.

I talked to an old sailor who was leaning on the rail beside me. I told him that this was the first time I had ever been to sea, though I had always wanted to be a seaman. He stopped puffing his pipe, and looked at me as though I was stupid, saying, 'How the hell did you get over there, then?'

When we reached Southampton a special train, marked with its red cross, was waiting alongside the quay. Voluntary workers pushed cigarettes into our mouths as we were carried away to the train, wishing us all well. The same thing happened at Basingstoke, before we ended up in Park Prewitt Hospital.

For the first time in seven days my foot was X-rayed. The injury was found to be in the spring ligament, and three days later I was transferred to Chester, along with the others, in a special train. At Liverpool we were taken through the Mersey

Tunnel to Upton Park Hospital, which had been intended for the mentally sick and had padded cells running off the ward we were in.

The only treatment was cold compresses, applied every few hours. It took a further week before the swelling went down. I was allowed to get dressed and hobble about the ward between sessions at the physio department. A week later I ventured out into the grounds.

While walking beside some shrubs, I heard a voice coming from behind them, calling me to come over. I went behind the bushes to find a tall fence, and a woman looking through the railings. She asked me if I was coming to the dance tonight, and I replied that just at the moment I was having difficulty even in walking. Then I noticed another woman walking along pretending to read a book, and two more were standing on a seat shouting something, and at last the penny dropped!

There was nothing wrong with the nurses, especially a little French nurse who looked after our ward. Four of us used to torment her whenever she came near. One morning, while she was tidying the bed, I pulled her across it, lifted her dress and spanked her bottom, but she took it all as good fun. I remember she had a lovely pair of silk pants on. I was the only patient who was mobile, and spent a lot of time in the ward office doing little jobs: folding dressings, etc. However, our Nurse was courting, and would not have anything to do with me outside the ward.

Then came the time when three of us could wear hospital blues, white shirt and red tie. We were allowed to wear our own berets and could go into Chester. It was Saturday, so we had a walk round the shops, and I called in to a tobacconist near an archway over the road with a large clock on it. It was difficult to buy cigarettes or tobacco unless you were a regular customer at a shop, so I was surprised when not only did they give me tobacco, but a pipe also (from under the counter, of course). We had our lunch in the British Home Stores self service, or it may have been Littlewoods, and, while we were waiting at the checkout to pay for it, the Manager came and put his hand over the till, waiving payment. We were beginning to like Chester very much!

Only allowed out until 7pm, we decided to make the most of it by seeing a film and went along to the Odeon, and as we joined the queue for the 1/9d seats, the Manager came along and invited us into the best seats, which were in the dress circle. We could not get over the many kindnesses we were receiving. The city boasts a beautiful cathedral so on Sunday I went along to the service. As I was leaving, an old lady pressed two half crowns into my hand and then disappeared into the crowd. The people of Chester were so very kind to the soldiers from the hospital.

My foot was improving, and the hospital staff said I could go on seven days' leave. I was soon telephoning the lady next door to my home, and I heard her shouting to my mother as she came through the special gate between the gardens. Very pleased, she said she would bake some of my favourite cakes, and I am sure that she had saved up rations so that I could eat well when I came home. The journey from the west is a slow one, and I had to change trains at Leeds.

I shared a compartment with some WAAFS who had been posted to Thornaby. They wanted to know what sort of a place Stockton was, and Middlesbrough. Just before the train pulled into Thornaby Station, one of them put her arms round my neck and started kissing me as if it would save her life. The train stopped, and the Sergeant in charge of the WAAFS was holding the door open, shouting at her to get a move on, and the girl was in tears and hanging on to me for all she was worth. The Guard appeared, to see what the delay was. I had to get out of the train, half carrying the girl, before she would let go. It was a very strange situation, and for once I was glad to get back into a carriage on my own!

As I walked into Middlesbrough, I was looking at all the familiar places as if I had never seen them before. I felt privileged to be home, safe and well, and I could not help thinking of all my friends who would not be going home ever again. I had changed, and mentally matured, there was no doubt about that, during the last three months in Normandy.

The first person I met was an old pal from my school days, Denis Hickman, who lived in the next road. He asked me if I had seen any Germans in France! I told him I had seen one or two. He was eighteen, the same age as me, but already I had a wealth of experience he could not understand, and probably never would.

It was lovely seeing my folks again, but I realised that even they had no idea what I had been doing since they last saw me. My values had changed considerably, but I was pleased that they could carry on in their own sweet way, as they had always done. During my leave the Ist Division dropped into Arnhem and I followed every move they made as the news came over the radio, knowing only too well what they were going through. I had had some horrible experiences, and used to dream about them, and one night I must have been shouting in my sleep and woke everybody up. I even woke our neighbours, yet my nerves were in good shape as far as I knew.

As soon as my friend Bill Monahan heard that I was home, he brought his record-player for me to use while I was on leave. He was always thoroughly reliable, and had the same qualities that I recognised in Ron Sturdy. A local dance hall was the meeting-place of a group of friends whom I saw when home on leave. Bill and I went along.

Dorothy was also there, having every dance with the same chap. Bill, who knew me better than anyone, said, 'Go on - ask her for a dance.' I declined. Later on he reminded me that it was almost the last dance, saying, 'Don't you think she would dance with you?'

'Of course she would!' I assured him, but he challenged me to prove it.

I made my way across the floor to where she was sitting with her friend. I was nearing them when they got up and were about to start dancing. I did wonder if my offer would get a refusal, but it was accepted. I have no idea what happened to her friend, or to Bill either; from that moment on we had eyes only for each other.

Suddenly I was on top of the world, and my life had a new meaning. Although I had thought a lot about Iris in Southampton, I realised that I had always been in love with Dorothy.

That week I met Harry and May, Dorothy's parents, and found them wonderful company. On that very night there was an air raid, and we all moved into the shelter. When the anti-aircraft guns opened fire, Dorothy started to shake – I could hardly believe that she was so badly affected. The close encounter a few doors away had left her in a nervous state.

Harry recalled an incident which had happened just three years earlier, and had us all in tears of laughter. Dorothy had an uncle called Fred who was over forty and a bachelor, who loved a joke. Almost every day he would tease the life out of some member of the family. He played the flute in the local orchestra, and one night he had come in late from a concert. At that time of the war, an invasion was on everyone's mind, and there had been a lot of talk about German Parachutists.

The Germans had dropped land mines, quite large bombs which came down slowly by parachute. A few people had had a terrible shock, thinking they were the start of the invasion. Just as Fred turned into Albert Terrace, he got just such a shock. Only 5' 4" and weighing under eight stone, he felt helpless and terrified, and ran as fast as he could. Everyone was in bed after having spent the night before in the shelter, and had turned in long before 11pm. Racing up the stairs, Fred made as much noise as possible.

'They are here, they are here, get up quick!' he shouted, dashing from room to room.

The whole family were now in a blind panic. Harry said, 'What the hell's the matter, waking us all up?'

'It's the bloody Germans: they are here; there's a parachute in the trees at the back of our house.'

Harry was out of bed and into his trousers in three seconds flat. He raced down the stairs, followed by the rest of the family, and out into the back garden.

Harry grabbed a spade. 'Where are the bastards?' They all peered up into the trees. 'That's not a parachute, you fool!' Harry was furious. 'It's the barrage balloon: it's broken loose from its moorings in Albert Park.'

Fred did nothing but laugh, and for years afterwards the story brought laugher to people; Harry never let him live it down, either.

*

My leave came to an end and I was back with the 9th Para again. It was great to see a few old faces returning after hospital treatment, but there was an amazing amount of new ones. The new Paras had joined us to bring the Battalion back up to the strength of 650. Training commenced furiously. The 1st Division had been cut to pieces at Arnhem, and any emergency would now fall on the 6th Division, the only Airborne troops available from the British forces.

I was enjoying a regular supply of letters from Dorothy, and living for my next leave. News of a Christmas leave gave us much to look forward to. My second birthday in the Battalion was almost due, when I would attain the age of nineteen; already I was a veteran with battle experience which now had to be conveyed to the new recruits. Our exercises were endless, but the training was paying off, the battalion was taking shape, and the floors in the barrack rooms were highly polished.

In the NAAFI we made our own entertainment. Two London lads could take off Flanagan and Allen so well that they could earn as much beer as they could drink every night.

There was a competition to see which barrack room could make the best impression when the CO inspected us one Saturday morning. The winning company would get a head start, as leave passes would be given to them first. We decorated a Christmas tree, and placed some imitation dog dirt in our rivals' toilet area, to ensure a satisfactory result.

The surprise was total: instead of being inspected, we were paraded in the main dining hall for the CO, Lieutenant-Colonel Crookenden, to speak to us. We had heard the news on the radio about the Ardennes break-through, but had thought the Yanks could deal with it. Monty had called on us to stand by. We heard that the Super Tiger tanks which the Panzers were using had extra armour plating, and the allies did not have a gun capable of stopping them. Rumour had it (falsely) that we would be dropped a few miles in front of them, dig in and get them with gammon bombs from behind after they passed over us. We could make our own gammon bombs by squeezing several sticks of plastic explosive into a sock type of container with a fuse, and throwing them. They were very effective.

Rumours were running wild, but the only thing we were sure about was that all leave had been cancelled, and everyone was feeling pretty low. We went back to the barrack room, and someone let off steam by throwing a boot from one end of the room to the other. It came back, with a chair, and then a bed. Everyone had gone mad. The decorations came down and the smart room was turned into a shambles in just a few minutes. A stirrup pump was brought into action, but not to be outdone a hose-pipe was fixed in retaliation and drowned the pump crew. Eventually the cold water brought us all to our senses and we had to clean up the mess before going to the NAAFI.

A special train took us to Dover the following day, and we waited our turn to cross to Calais. It came the next morning: Christmas Day 1944, at 8am. We had our Christmas meal on the docks at Calais, and it consisted of two tinned sausages, powdered potatoes, and two German cigars as a special treat.

Chapter 10

In the Ardennes and on the Maas

Transport took us into Belgium, to the town of Ghent, and 'C' Company ended up in a monastery. A foot of snow had fallen and the toilets across the yard were frozen solid; we had one blanket and a groundsheet each, and the floors in the monastery were sandstone slabs.

The Battalion was once again awaiting its instructions to move up front. In the mean time we tried to keep warm. Next morning Harry Bedford and I had a walk down the road, where we met two children. When we asked them where we could find a café, they pointed to a house and went with us to the door. It was their home, and their mother, Madame Des Camps, invited us in. She could speak very good English, and her maid brought us coffee and biscuits and we talked non stop.

It was soon dinner time, so we made a move to go, but then Dr Des Camps arrived. He, too, spoke excellent English, and we stayed to dinner. They told us about their illegal radio, which could pick up the BBC during the occupation. They were very worried indeed that General Von Runstead's breakthrough was heading their way, just like in 1914 and 1940: the Germans always made for Ghent and then Antwerp Port. We assured them that we would stop them before they got anywhere near Ghent, but the women-folk cried just the same. These people were so very kind: they offered us a bedroom with twin beds and a wash basin, which was wonderful. Permission had to be given before we could accept, but the Sergeant Major, Sid Knight, said that as long as we attended roll call at 8am it was all right.

We took the family some soap, and chocolates for the children. That night we had a meal to remember, with a different wine for each course, starting with soup and ending with coffee and a brandy. They seemed to be quite a wealthy family, but their cook-maid was treated as one of the family really and sat down to eat with us: they were lovely people. We had one more day with them, then were told that transport would be taking us into the Ardennes forest the next day. When we left at 7am, the whole family was in tears, including the maid, and they hugged and kissed us goodbye.

It was snowing when we moved off in convoy towards the Ardennes, and by mid afternoon we were approaching Namur on the river Meuse. People were pushing hand carts and cycles, all piled up with their belongings, prams, or anything on wheels, toward Brussels. When they saw all the red berets, truck-loads of us, they stopped and cheered and waved until we were almost out of sight. The next time we looked back, they had turned round and were going back to their homes! It seemed that the Belgian people had more faith in us than in the Americans.

Late on the day before New Year's Eve, the 9th Battalion moved into another monastery, the Abbeye de Maredsous. We used the monks' dining hall to eat in, and I believe that our cooks went to work in the monks' kitchens. There were several sittings, and after each meal the monks cleaned down the stone tables and helped in every way. On one table the monks had several attractive trinkets and crosses. I bought some for my cousin Margaret, who was a Catholic, and a cross for myself.

The day was spent checking our equipment. The 13th Battalion had moved up ahead of us, and we had to leave first thing on New Year's Day, to try and make contact with the Boche. At about 11pm I walked into the Abbey; it was so quiet in there, and dark, apart from a few candles burning. In one corner was a manger, with two little figures about a foot high. I sat there all alone for two hours, praying for all the people back home and asking that I might see them all again, in one piece. The atmosphere was so peaceful that it was difficult to believe that only a few miles away terrible things were happening. I left the Abbey, feeling much better for the experience.

As the Battalion was lined up outside next morning, the Abbot came round and blessed the crosses which had been purchased; he said prayers for all of us before we got into the transport, then we moved on up the road to Dinant, and an hour later were on the forest road.

We pushed on into the hills among some very tall pine trees, the snow being very deep in places where it had drifted. Soon we came across evidence of some bitter fighting. It was so cold that the wounds on the dead Germans did not bleed, and they appeared to have frozen soon after death, with their skin glazed like marble or wax. There was one with the bottom of his jaw shot away completely, leaving his top teeth protruding, but there was hardly any blood on his uniform. The temperature was around 25°F below. One of his arms was sticking out, and the lads shook his hand as they passed his body, making some unprintable remark about being on parade without his bottom teeth in.

We dropped down on to a road leading to a village called Humain. Around this village both German and American equipment was laid about. A Tiger tank had 'brewed up' close to the tangled, twisted seventeen-pounder anti-tank gun and crew near by. There was a scout car, riddled with bullets and covered with blood, also two snipers in a burned-out haystack, who had been burned beyond all recognition alongside their machine-gun. Most of the buildings in the village were damaged, but we occupied them for cover that night.

A little further to our right, the 13th Battalion were involved in what was called later one of the toughest battles of the Ardennes campaign, at a place called Bures. They suffered very heavy casualties, but stopped the German advance with the assistance of the 12th Battalion and the 29th Armoured Brigade. 'C' Company of the 13th Para was commanded by Major Clark MC. Affectionately known as 'Nobby', he first joined the Life Guards in 1925, and became an Airborne soldier in 1940. The house he occupied in Bures received a direct hit, and Nobby was blown out of a window and lost his sight.

Weeks later in hospital, he regained his sight and from that moment on he took a great interest in religion. After leaving the Army, in which he had commanded an Airborne training camp as Colonel, he became a Deacon in Salisbury Cathedral, and later a missionary in Lahore, Pakistan, where he lived in a mud hut for a number of years.

Returning to England, he joined the Prison Service as a Chaplain, and served at Liverpool and Parkhurst, where at the time some of the great train robbers were doing their penance. Nobby's next move was to Windsor Castle as a Military Knight. He enjoyed his life there, and loved showing friends the Queen's quarters and gardens from the roof of his house. He attended many reunions and conducted services at Ranville in Normandy and Hooten in the Ardennes. He was a man much loved by all who knew him. Sadly, he died in 1991 at the age of 85.

Before leaving Humain, our Padre, John Gwinnett, had an organ pulled from a damaged house into the street, and we held a short service while one of the boys played hymns on the organ. Just before the service was over, some 88mm shells came over, but they missed us by half a mile.

Moving off into the forest again, we continued our search for live Germans, but found only dead ones. Several miles on, but still in the forest, we took up our usual all-round protection position, but could not dig in, for the ground was so hard that it was impossible to dig the earth beneath the snow. We still had our one blanket and a ground sheet which we doubled up, making up sleeping-bag types of beds. At first light we tried folding up the blankets, but they just snapped like biscuits.

Our company truck arrived close by with some hot tea: one mug each. We had to share one mug to drink and another to shave; everyone had to shave. Brigadier James Hill came round to see us and said we had had 26°F of frost that night. My eyelids had frozen together, and I could not open them till I held warm hands to the lashes.

Off we went again, moving down a forest track leading on to a road. We continued for a few miles before arriving at a village called Bande. We did not see any men there, only women folk who told us that the Germans had pulled out yesterday and taken all the men to work in Germany. 'A' Company pressed on down the road, 'B' Company went off into the area each side of the village and 'C' Company moved into buildings for accommodation. My section was sent to a small house on the right as we entered the main street. We were using the downstairs rooms. I took a look upstairs and found an old lady, two young women and their eight children. They were carefully serving a meal of potatoes boiled in their jackets. We returned a few minutes later with tinned meat, soap and chocolates. When they saw what we had put down on the table, their faces said everything.

'A' Company reported finding a café cellar two miles away with bodies dumped in on top of one another; they had all been shot in the back of the head. They were the male population of Bande village. Each body was brought back and laid out for identification, and next day we provided transport to the Cemetery, where they were buried in a mass grave.

My platoon took up a standing patrol in the woods three miles east of Bande. We lay in the snow from first light to dusk and, during this time, deer came within 20 yards of us. This indicated that the woods were clear of the Boche, and in fact they had been retreating at great speed.

The platoon left the village next morning early, making for a farm some miles away through the forest. It was completely deserted but the pigs and hens were still running around. We found some corn and fed them, and then prepared our own meal. On the following morning, one man had been detailed to have a meal ready for us when we returned that night. There was a large boiler and plenty of wood and some turnips; he could stoke up the boiler and get cracking!

The platoon set off back into the forest looking for the Boche, who had fled the area, of course, a day or so earlier; still, we had to make sure. At our return, just before darkness fell, we were very hungry indeed, and the smell from the boiler was lovely as we lined up with our mess tins and each took a turn to dip into the chicken stew.

As we all sat around eating, a voice suddenly shouted to the cook of the day, 'Didn't you cut the hen's feet off before putting it in the boiler?' This was followed by, 'No, he didn't cut its head off either: I've got it.' By this time the lads were fishing out feathers from the stew. It appeared that he had just caught the fowls and thrown them straight into the boiling water with some turnips and potatoes and salt. He was never asked to cook again!

We decided to kill a pig, and Private White, an ex-butcher, said he would prepare it. Three pigs were running free in a large pen, each one about the size of a large dog. They would not stay still long enough for anyone to take careful aim with a ·45 pistol, but several shots later one of them fell to the ground, shot through the head. Private White hung the animal on a barn door and cut it open and cleaned it out. He said it would be three days before we could eat the meat, however. Next morning he said it was satisfactory as, owing to the extremely cold weather, the blood had frozen, and we could eat it. On returning that night, each of us had a large, thick pork chop, and it was very tasy indeed.

Two days later the Americans took over from us; after all, it was their sector. We moved into Holland, which was only a day's truck drive away, arriving at a village called Horn. There was still a foot of snow lying there, and we moved into houses around the village. A straight road ran toward the river Maas, built high up from the ground with two dykes passing under it. The road was lined with trees for nearly two miles before reaching the river and a steel bridge, which the enemy had destroyed after they had crossed. They were occupying the town of Roermond on the other side of the Maas.

Just before the bridge, on the right-hand side, was a brick works and a smaller road leading to a farm house a mile further on, which stood a few hundred yards from the river. This was to be our FOP (forward observation post). It was manned by a platoon on 48 hours duty at a time. We covered the windows with hessian, which allowed us to see out, but not a movement within could be detected. Up in the roof we lifted a couple of tiles an inch, giving us a perfect view of the German positions across the river. At each corner of the farm buildings, which formed a square with a yard area in the centre, we removed three bricks from each wall along the same course, just above ground level, dug a machine-gun post in each corner, and placed in it a Bren gun. Each one had 90° of field fire.

A passage leading from the back of the buildings was lined with pig sties, three at each side. On arriving, one of the members of the platoon tried to get water from the pump. Had he been a little more experienced, he would not have touched it until it had been properly inspected. The rest of the platoon's new members learned a terrible lesson well, when they saw the lad blown to pieces. A booby trap fitted to the handle of the pump was attached to a mortar bomb hidden in the pump lagging. Most of us who had been in Normandy had seen the tricks the Boche would get up to, and did not touch anything, not even dead bodies, till we had made a close inspection.

Getting to one corner gun position involved crawling through a haystack along a tunnel we had made through it. Each time we crawled along it, the rats would complain, squeaking as loud as they could. These gun positions were manned for two hours, before a change-over in daylight. For one hour at dusk and dawn everyone was on guard duty, then, during darkness, half the platoon was on duty for one hour and would then take an hour's rest before changing over again. We called this a 50% stand-to.

We found that the farmer's wife had been very industrious, for the shelves in the cellar were full of bottled fruit and meat of every kind: plums, strawberries, raspberries, also pickled eggs and home-made sausages. In fact, we had some really good meals during our stay at this post, and there was a very lucky find for me. I recognised a sewing machine as being the same make as my mother's. She had been unable to get a new needle for hers since the war had started. I removed the needle and stuck it in my pay book, and it did fit and she was able to carry on working with it.

Our 48-hour duty was over and 13 Platoon arrived an hour after dark to relieve us. It was normal for us to move about in darkness, unlike the Boche, who changed over in daylight and would get shelled by our guns on our instructions. We moved on down the road to the brick works, then along the straight road back to Horn. The Germans had heavy machine-guns trained on this road, and the only cover was from the trees. There was only a split second to dash behind the trees once the guns opened fire and the red tracer bullets came dancing along the road, spreading out more the further they travelled.

Just before the village of Horn a large hessian screen was hung between the trees, so that no movement in the streets could be observed from Roermond during the day. There was a more relaxed atmosphere back in Horn during our 72-hour stay, before it was our turn again to man the FOP. Guards were active outside each billet during the night. One night, one of the guards was about to relieve his friend and thought he would play a trick on him, creeping up behind him in the early hours. The guard turned round and shot him. He was perfectly justified in doing so, but when he found it was his pal he was terribly upset. The new boys had learned another bitter lesson that night.

Back at the FOP there had been some excitement when a German patrol had crossed the river Maas by boat. They wore white suits in the snow. One of them came through the alley way leading into the yard; he heard the pigs snoring and thought they were troops. He fired his automatic into the pigsty, killing all the pigs but one. George Basher raced to the other end of the passage, opening fire on the German. He might have killed him, as there were blood traces on the snow, but he must have been carried away. One of the Bren guns opened fire on the intruders before they left the area; but the Boche had placed an explosive charge against the wall of the farmhouse and it killed two lads on the other side of it.

It was the turn of 12th Platoon to man the FOP. The weather was extremely cold, and rum rations were issued. I was sent down to the Observation Post with five lads carrying a large demi-john of rum for 12th Platoon, with some ammunition. I took my water bottle to collect rum for the patrol from the Quartermaster. It was half full - but the best was yet to come. When I arrived to issue it to the other members of the patrol, no-one liked rum, so I kept the six-man ration. It was very strong, like Navy rum, and I kept having a swig.

The journey to the FOP was uneventful and the machine-guns did not open fire. Sergeant Johnson told me that the Boche had come over and crawled up to the house in their white suits. The Bren gun was handled, but nothing had happened as it was frozen solid. The Sergeant rolled a hand-grenade through the slits in the wall, and he thought that at least one German left blood in the snow, but there were no bodies when daylight came. He advised me to keep a sharp look-out on the way back - not that I needed much warning - as the Boche were coming across the river every night in small patrols.

We began moving back down the lane leading to the brick works, when I noticed the sound of rushing water; then suddenly it reached us and almost knocked us over. In seconds we could see only water, where just previously the ground had been white with snow. It now reached my knees, and was icy cold, but we stood still while I got my bearings. The lane was no longer visible and, although I could see the brick works, or the outline of it, we could only move very slowly towards it, putting one foot in front of the other.

The farm was on high ground and was not affected by the flooding, but one of the patrol put a foot wrong in the water-covered lane and went down in the ditch beside it. At last we arrived at the brick works where, as we passed the kilns, the water became less deep; we went up some steps and on to the road which was quite dry. I took another sip of the magic rum, which brought me back to life, and we stepped out on the last two miles to Horn.

The Company Commander, Ian Dyer, was anxious to report the news of the flooding to Brigade Headquarters, giving details of its depth and the strength of its flow, etc. Next day it was reported that the dams had been opened, up river, by the enemy, to flood the Maas and deny us access to the low ground. The accuracy of this report must have impressed someone, because only two days later I was told to put on another stripe, making me a full Corporal.

Major Dyer had a brilliant idea. He called all the officers and NCO's together to a meeting, and we listened intently as he demonstrated his naval expertise. It seemed logical to us that, to visit the FOP, all we had to do was to sail on a certain compass reading for 'x' number of yards, then alter course to another reading for a further number of yards, and we should reach the Post by 01.45 hours - simple. The flat-bottomed boats arrived next morning, and we fixed them by lifting the gunwales and pushing ribs hinged to the bottom of the boats under them. The canvas sides remained upright and tight, making the job look easy. There was an ample supply of paddles, so it was all arranged for that night: we were to visit the FOP by boat.

Major Dyer and six NCO's went in the first boat, and Platoon Commander Lieutenant Jock Lepper and six NCO's including me, in the second. The boats were easily carried along the road to the water's edge, the officers going in front with the compass, and each of the crew carrying a yard-long paddle. We pushed off on one bearing for 500 yards. All went well, considering none of us had done this kind of thing before; we developed an orderly rhythm and the Navy would have been proud of us. All of a sudden a great black object came up out of the water and was heading towards us. It passed very close but we could not identify it. Then, just as quickly, something similar whizzed by.

'Hell!' someone shouted. 'That was a tree.'

It was our boat that was tearing along, not the tree! Everything was pitch black, both water and sky, and we had no idea what was happening until we heard the roar of water in the distance. The noise got louder, rushing like a waterfall. Then the Germans sent up a flare, and we got our bearings, staying completely still and hoping they would not see us and fire upon us with their machine-guns. The boats continued to race along, heading for the dykes under the road to Roermond. The turbulence sounded violent as the water rushed towards one of the dykes, and it was a very frightening experience to be carried helplessly in the fast-moving current.

As we were paddling furiously to get out of the main stream, suddenly the boat heeled over and we all landed on one side. It had hit a barbed-wire fence. We grabbed hold and managed to hang on and, up to our chests in the freezing cold water, we slowly eased the boat along the fence toward the road and embankment. It took half an hour to move it the 50 yards, and for the last few yards we dragged it. On reaching the road we tipped the boat on its side to get rid of the water, and sat on the embankment to pull ourselves together.

The other boat had gone out of sight, but later we discovered that the crew had had a similar experience; somehow they managed to do a recovery job, saving their boat and weapons. We carried the boats back up the road to reach Horn three hours after leaving, feeling and looking like drowned rats. When he saw the state we were in, the old man in whose house my section was billeted said, 'Nix godd ower da Maas tonight.' It came to be a catch phrase in the Company and gave us many a laugh. That night the rum ration was most welcome.

Next day, one of the young mothers had just hung out her washing on the line between two apple trees, and two little children were looking out of the windows, when we heard the unmistakable sound of a German 88mm shell on its way. We rushed to pull the little ones away from the windows, and seconds later a great lump of shrapnel came through the window and embedded itself in the wall opposite. The washing was down in the snow, but no-one was hurt.

Every day we ran around in the snow in our bare feet for ten minutes. It improved the circulation and prevented 'trench foot', and as a result not one case was reported in the Division during the whole Ardennes campaign, while the Americans had lots of casualties from this complaint during the same period. Trench foot was a dreadful thing: the feet went black and the toes dropped off.

It was our turn again to relieve the lads at the FOP. The water was going down but the ground was still covered a foot deep, even a mile from the river. The farm was high and dry, and we changed our socks immediately we arrived, making ourselves feel a little more comfortable.

The large surviving pig had become a pet. It was allowed to roam anywhere in the yard, and slept in the same straw-lined room we used when off duty. A large sack of corn was opened, and the pig just ate and slept until he was hungry again. During the night, when we changed over duty every hour, it was always a mad rush to be back at the rest room first, so that we could sleep next to the pig: he was always lovely and warm.

These duties went on for two more weeks, and by the time we handed over to the Americans once again, in mid February, the water had gone down a good deal. However, they could not have found one jar of eatables in the cellar, as we had taken care of those! A few chickens still roamed around at their own risk, and there was still plenty of pork to cut at, which the Germans had provided for us when they shot the pigs. In fact we had become sick of having pork day after day.

Trucks arrived to take us to an airfield, and Dakotas flew us back to our own local airfield at Netheravon at long last. We had seven days leave, and it was heaven to be home again.

Chapter 11

The Drop over the Rhine

On our return to Bulford, we found an excercise was planned involving the whole Division. It was to be a mass drop: six battalions of Para dropping at the same time near Oxford, close to the Thames, which was to represent the Rhine. The British Second Army stood at the side of the Rhine near Wesel, and our next operation was to be there.

Monty had the 51st Highland Division and the 1st Commando Brigade in formation near the river. On the German side the area was defended by their 1st Parachute Army, the 86th Corps Infantry and the 57th Panzer Corps. They had positioned field artillery on high ground, a bank of wooded country overlooking the river where they expected a crossing to be made. They had made every farm house, cottage and barn into a stronghold. The German Parachute Commander knew that there would be an airborne landing, and the only thing not known to him was the date and time. He decided that the 'planes and gliders would have to be hit in the air before they landed. He was not short of anti-aircraft guns, and emplacements were quickly established.

A continuous smokescreen covered the movements of the British, who had assembled DUKW's, Buffalo and Naval craft on trailers, parked at numerous assembly areas. Tanks, guns and ammunition were in supply, ready for the first move. This time there would be no scattering of the Division in the dark, as in our Normandy operation. We would drop directly on to the enemy in broad daylight. What was daunting was, that the area was defended by German paratroops, who were considered the best troops in the German army. They would fight to the last man. The Gliders would follow us a few minutes later with their anti-tank guns, to deal with the Panzers.

The exercise went well, and it was a wonderful sight to see so many planes and 'chutes in the air all at one time. The preparation for the real thing went ahead furiously, and we were all ready by well into March 1945. On the 16th we moved off to Essex in special trains. The Division would be taking off from Chipping Ongar, Boreham and Weatherfield, all RAF stations.

It was the usual practice to send all our personal things home before an operation. In view of the distress my mother would encounter on receiving them, I decided to send mine to Dorothy. I would be unable to explain why I had sent them, and she too would worry and wonder what was going on; but the news would be out anyway once the operation had been reported.

Lieutenant Mc Guffie joined 14 Platoon, taking over from Jock Lepper, who had been promoted to Captain. Mc Guffie was a nice chap and got on well with the members of his platoon. His favourite word was 'organised', and whenever he gave his orders he would follow them up with, 'Get organised!'. He quickly became known to us all as 'The Organiser'.

We studied models and photographs. The 9th Battalion had the job of destroying the artillery on the high ground. The 1st Canadian Battalion had to clear the Germans on the DZ, so that we could get on with our job as soon as possible. The 8th Battalion had to get rid of as many anti-aircraft guns as they could; it was estimated that there were over 800 batteries. Two hundred and forty-two Dakotas would carry us to Germany on the 24th March and we would drop at 10am.

It was a fine morning; we were on the airfield by 5.30am, and at 7am the first 'plane took off. Soon we were rolling down the runway. A 'buzz bomb' (a V1) passed over our heads on its way to London. It took us an hour's flying around to form up into Vs. Passing over the coastline, we had an escort of 200 Spitfires from Fighter Command. The sun was shining, and we could see the coast of Belgium below. Lines of aircraft in front and behind seemed endless, and it was the most wonderful sight. It was an exciting thought that this was the largest airborne operation ever seen. The journey took three hours, but it was very interesting, because I spent every minute watching the flying going on on all sides. At the back of my mind I wondered what the next hour held for us. We knew it would be curtains for some of us! - but which ones?

The word came: twenty minutes to go. We checked our equipment, then stood up to fasten our hooks on to the steel wire above our heads, and we watched for the red and green lights above the door. I was jumping last but one. Sergeant

BIRRELL

Scott was last. He was married to a girl from Stockton and was much older than any of us: he had been in India before the war started.

The river Rhine was very wide and the sun was reflecting on it as we passed over. The Commandos had gone across during the night to capture Wesel, and the Highland Divisions would be doing their best to get across under a smoke-screen. Our arrival should be helping them, as it seemed that every gun in the German army was now firing at us!

The red light was on; now the green - and out goes the first lad. We lose no time and follow on very quickly. Suddenly the 'plane heels over and some lads fall down, weighted heavily with equipment. It is difficult to get up quickly, but they do, and jumping continues. As I move down towards the door, red flames are passing the windows on my left, and I can feel the heat through the side of the plane.

The starboard engine was on fire, but we all managed to get out. I was pleased to feel my 'chute open with a tug at the shoulders, and the cool air was welcome. Checking my 'chute, I noticed small holes appearing; the enemy could not wait for us to get down; of course they knew as well as we did that a Para is helpless until he get his rifle or automatic in his hands. Our 'plane was leaving a trail of black smoke, but had held a steady course.

BIRRELL

I was coming down at the extreme end of the DZ, in fact Sergeant Scott would land beyond it, on the other side of a railway in some woods. The noise was deafening: heavy guns firing at the 'planes still coming over, and small arms everywhere. I opened my clasp knife, ready to cut my rifle free, and saw a group of Germans firing from the railway embankment at two of our lads, who were landing 100 yards away as I lowered my rifle valise 25 feet below me. A ploughed field coming up should make a soft landing, just missing the railway, but uncomfortably close to the Boche with their automatics and a machine-gun. A perfect landing! and record time losing my 'chute and swinging the haversack on my back, from the position on the chest which was used for jumping.

Racing towards the valise, I was conscious of the machine-gun firing and was flung like a paper bag in the opposite direction for at least three yards. Without thinking, I jumped to my feet and again raced towards the rifle, diving down with my knife in my hand to cut the stitching. The machine-gun opened fire again, showering me with soil and dust as the bullets hit the ground half a yard in front of me. I had slashed a good few stitches when it fired again; this time my hand went numb, the knife disappeared completely and fragments had cut into my face - I could feel the blood running down it. At least my eyes were all right.

There was absolutely nothing I could do, so I stayed perfectly still. The next burst from the MG42 would be right on target. I fully expected to die, and my mind travelled through my past life at a terrific rate. I saw flashes in my mind of myself as a child of three or four years old with my parents, then instantaneously my age jumped to eight and ten and so on until the last leave. I remember thinking, 'People will never know how it happened'; then, just as though I had woken up, it dawned on me that I was still alive.

Other lads were coming down, and 'planes were passing overhead. I heard a machine-gun open up, but nothing came my way; the enemy must have thought I was dead. One of the Canadian Para lads was moving along towards the nest of German Para below the embankment, in dead ground, as we called it, out of their view. He got close enough to throw a grenade into their midst; without waiting for it to explode, I jumped up and ran towards our RV, which was in the opposite direction. In less than 100 yards a hedge crossed the field, and I dived over it into a ditch.

The first man I saw was the Bren gunner from my section, who handed over his revolver, a ·45, to me. I put a field dressing on my hand, he tied it up, and we then moved along the ditch towards our RV. We crossed over some open ground into a small wooded area. Some of the 8th Battalion lads were there, and had six Germans lined up. We were told that everyone who landed in the trees beyond the railway line had been shot immediately on landing, including their Padre with his red cross arm-band. The Commanding Officer of the Canadian Para and Sergeant ~~Scott~~ had suffered the same fate, when they landed on the other side of the railway.

We left the 8th Battalion lads with the prisoners and bashed on to meet the rest of the 9th at the RV. The noise was still terrific, with explosions, and the roar of aircraft above, releasing the gliders. One glider had been hit, and came down from 1,000 feet like confetti. Another 'plane was losing height with an engine on fire. We moved along quickly, but the next second a glider shot past us at 80mph, smashing into trees and breaking up in front of us. We reached the spot in seconds. Inside, our medical sergeant and his two orderlies were dead,

BIRRELL

the pilot had been killed, and under the glider, a Horsa, three more lads had been run down.

We could see the blue smoke indicating 'C' Company RV, and reported in. From 14 Platoon, only Sergeant Creasey and I had arrived, along with eighteen men. Three sergeants, two corporals and sixteen privates were missing. Reports were coming in of 35 gliders shot down and 18 Dakotas. Casualties were very heavy, because the German artillery were firing at point-blank range as the gliders landed and came to rest.

We split the Platoon into two sections and Sergeant Creasey and I led one each. He moved off from the RV, followed by Lieutenant Mc Guffie and his Runner, and my section brought up the rear. The Battalion moved off to find high ground and put the enemy artillery out of action. Checking myself, I found that four bullets had hit me when I was knocked over. Three had gone into my small pack, cutting through mess tins, rations, a spare pair of socks and a towel, all of which were ruined. The fourth bullet had gone through my right-hand ammunition pouch, missed two '36' grenades and a phosphorus grenade, cut into smock and battledress and, passing through shirt and pullover, had hit the cross in my breast pocket.

This cross, along with identity discs, had usually been worn round my neck ever since the visit to the Abbeye de Maredsous in the Ardennes the previous December. However, the rush to get to parade early that morning had caused me to put it in my breast pocket, just to save time. Up to the moment of discovering the cross, the adrenalin had been bubbling in my veins since we arrived at the DZ. Suddenly I was on top of the world: this cross had saved my life! The feeling was indescribable. There was no doubt in my mind whatsoever that I would never be hurt again. It was fantastic: I felt as if I had armour plating around me and that nothing could penetrate it. The more I thought about it, the better I felt, and it quickly dawned on me that, although my hand was full of splinters from the knife and looked terrible, there was hardly any pain at all. Prayer had always meant a lot to me, but I suppose that doubt had crept into my thinking. No longer had I any doubts about God and his understanding. I had lost every ounce of fear.

Moving into a field, we found a Horsa glider lying on its back, a total wreck. Inside was a jeep and a six-pounder anti-tank gun. The three gunners were dead among the carnage. We could hear the artillery pieces firing, and made straight for them, climbing up among the trees to their positions. Some German infantry got in the way and were quickly dealt with. Then we saw them: the line of heavy guns, so close together that the wheels were almost touching. We only shouted out and charged them with our bayonets, and the gunners put their hands up high and lined up at the double when we indicated they should do so. To me they looked like old men, but I suppose they would have been in their late twenties.

Leaving them with a couple of lads, off we dashed, on to the next bit of high ground, where we found yet another line of artillery, which had been pounding the lads trying to get across the Rhine a mile or so away. They too were quick to put up their hands, and caused little trouble. Two high-ranking officers came out of a bunker wearing long black overcoats. I dashed inside to see if there was anyone else in the command post; on the table lay two highly polished holsters, complete with fully loaded Lugers. The officers must have taken them from their belts before surrendering. I put them in my smock out of sight.

When I returned to the scene outside, one of the prisoners was being awkward. He looked an arrogant type, and was much younger than the others. It gave me more satisfaction to put my boot up his backside than if I had shot him. He moved, but not until he had turned and snarled at me but, whatever he was thinking, he must have changed his mind when he saw I was holding a ·45 in my left hand. We took the prisoners down into a quarry, with a guard to keep an eye on them. In all, 90 large pieces of artillery had been captured, from 70mm to 150mm. Now they no longer fired on the 15th Scottish as it crossed the Rhine.

A tank appeared near where Battalion HQ had grouped. The company clerk grabbed a PIAT anti-tank weapon and fired. The lid opened and the German crew jumped out and were killed. The tank was in good order, and was used by our lads, who painted a white star over the black cross.

At about 6pm a jeep came up to Battalion HQ and Monty stepped out, asking Colonel Crookenden where the enemy was now. The Colonel told the Chief, 'About 300 yards along this track.' Monty turned around and drove off. Later that night he sent a message to the Colonel's parents to say their son was well. The Colonel's father had served with Monty some years before. In the heat of a major operation, Monty had found the time to pass these reassuring words to worried parents.

The afternoon was creeping into dusk and, returning to the

high ground, we prepared to take over the enemy positions permanently. Major Dyer came round and seemed pleased with our day's work. Checking on the state of ammunition, casualties etc., he noticed my hand and sent me to the battalion aid post. It was eight hours since we had landed and there had been no time for food and drink, so the cup of sweet tea the medic gave me was most welcome. They put a dressing on the damaged hand, then I had some stew, which tasted great, then a shot in the arm. Just before I fell asleep on a ground sheet, I saw the red glow of jet engines pass over the tops of the trees. The Germans had jet fighters three months before the RAF's first jet was in operation.

Next morning the noise of tanks woke me. It was a lovely morning, the sun was shining and everyone seemed relaxed. The medics told me that the whole area was now clear of Boche, and the drive was soon to begin: a big push into the heart of Germany. Tanks rolled every few minutes as the 6th Guards armour joined in to help with the next stage of the job, but I was going another way, this time toward the Rhine and back to Holland.

Thirty of us who had been wounded the previous day crossed the river to waiting ambulances. Troops were still being ferried across the Rhine and there were convoys of vehicles, tanks and supplies, all waiting their turn. General Gale stood waiting for a lift across. When he saw red berets in the DUKW, he asked what it was like over there?

A sergeant said, 'It's quiet now, Sir.'

'Good', said General Gale, 'I'll go across then.' This was just typical Airborne humour, and it raised a laugh.

We all had a label pinned to our uniforms, with the details of injuries etc. Just a few miles down the road we reached No. 11 Field Dressing Station. The small convoy of ambulances was met by a team of medics and two doctors. They checked each one of us, asking if we were comfortable. One of the lads had to have his wound re-dressed, as it was soaked with blood. Then we moved on down the road quite a few miles, crossing the Dutch border to No. 12 FDS. We received the same treatment, so well organised that it must have given the badly injured great confidence. Hot tea was ready at each station, and remarks were written on our cards.

An hour's drive later, the convoy of ambulances pulled in to No. 81 British General Hospital, which was a Dutch monastery. My dressing was changed and a nurse showed me to a hall full of camp beds, where I was to sleep. She filled in a card to inform my parents that I was all right, but I knew they would still be worried. The card was already printed and the lines not applicable crossed out, so there was no way of enlarging on the details. It just said 'I have been wounded. I am in hospital.' Previously, we had all been allowed to write letters to be posted after we took off from Essex for the Rhine. I had told my mother not to worry about me, as I had asked God to keep me safe.

The news was out about the Rhine Crossing, but no details given about the cost of lives. The 6th Airborne had achieved all its objectives in twelve hours, but at considerable cost in men, 'planes and gliders.

Chapter 12

A Miracle and a Journey

It was about 6pm, the monks were singing in their chapel, and I sat at the back and listened to them for over an hour. I could not understand a word they were saying, but it sounded beautiful.

Reflecting on my experience in the DZ, it occurred to me that, had my cross not stopped the bullet, the injury would have been fatal, as it would have been impossible for any of the medics to get to me in time, or, in fact, for several hours. The wound would have been on the right side of the chest at the base of the rib cage. I went on to think that, if my hand had not become numb, I would have gone on cutting at the rifle valise; if, for instance it had been a leg wound, or any other wound but one in the hand, which was so effective in stopping my attempts at retaliation (it had even destroyed the knife so that there was nothing else for me to do but lie still), it would not have saved my life. One more burst from that machine gun, which had the correct range, would have riddled me with bullets: I would not have stood a chance.

Not a bone was damaged in my hand – and there are many; a bone could have been shattered, it could have meant losing my hand altogether. I had left a burning 'plane, had sat down in front of a machine-gun at 70 yards, I had escaped three bursts of bullets.

Over and over again, my thoughts confirmed my belief that I had experienced a miracle.

A colonel inspected our wounds next morning, and some of us were taken to an airfield, where a white Dakota with the red cross painted on its side took us to Brussels airport. Ambulances took the casualties to the British 111 General Hospital, quite a large building on the main road leading to Waterloo, the famous battlefield of the Iron Duke and Napoleon.

We were told to strip off and get a bath. I suppose I must

have looked scruffy enough, with mud and bloodstains on my trousers. My smock was torn and tattered in places, and inside it I was still hiding the two Lugers, fully loaded, which I had taken from the German officers in the bunker. The minute the Sister left us alone, I hid them under the mattress on the bed. She came back and, as she helped me to finish undressing, a piece of metal fell on the floor. It was the bullet that hit the cross: it had been still stuck to my shirt. She wanted to bath me, but I got in the bathroom first and slipped the bolt on.

'You can't wash yourself with one hand!' she was shouting.

But the noise of the taps drowned her voice, and I got on with it.

What a wonderful feeling, getting washed and into clean sheets! The only time that I had used a bed with sheets on was in hospitals, or on leave at home. The Sister came round with more of those cards to send home, to inform people of the new address. This time I sent them to Dorothy and to the Des Camps in Ghent, which is only a few hours' journey from Brussels.

A Canadian 1st Para, a sergeant 8th Para and I were sent to the theatre next morning. The Canadian had a chunk of shrapnel removed from his shoulder, and the Sergeant had his left leg amputated and came back to the ward singing all the naughty songs we were all familiar with: he was still under the anaesthetic. I was lucky, because the surgeon did not operate. Instead, he decided to leave the pieces in my hand, but to put it into a large mitt filled with the new wonder drug, penicillin. It felt very comfortable, and it was three weeks before they took it off.

The results were amazing: my hand came out, leaving almost all the pieces of knife blade and black plastic handle behind, and the half-inch gash had just about closed up. Each morning I had to report to the therapy department, where a nurse would sit with a pillow on her knee, resting my hand while she massaged it under a light. What a life! I could stand this for weeks, I thought.

Each morning there was a daily bed-making routine, and while this was going on I went to the bathroom with the two pistols under my dressing gown. I replaced them on my return, under the mattress. No-one knew of this little escapade, and luckily I was never found out.

Three of us had permission to leave the hospital and visit the town from 2pm till 6pm. Brussels is a lovely place, and the trams ran direct into the town from outside the hospital and travel was free. The Canadian and a tank driver and I got on a tram, and sat next to a chap who opened a small case and gave us each a new pack of playing cards. This was our first introduction to Brussels hospitality.

We wandered around a large department store, simply amazed at the goods on display. Fruits, sweets and confectionery were rationed at home. A small boy of eight or nine years was staring up at me, looking very puzzled. His mother came up and spoke quite good English: 'He wants to know which regiment you belong?' The hospital blues and white shirt were new to him. I took my cap badge from my beret and gave it to him, showing him the parachute on it. His mother had slipped away, and returned with a large brown paper bag, flung it into my arms, and made a hasty retreat. It contained sweets, cakes and fruit, etc.

Joining my pals, I walked with them down the street gazing into shop windows. The shops were full of things like watches and other items not seen at home since the war started. A gentleman came up to enquire if I knew of a relative who had been in England since 1940 and who was a Para. He insisted we join him for a drink in a café. 'Tea', I thought; but cafés on the Continent serve any kind of drink, and after suitable refreshment and a chat we bade him goodbye.

It was decided that, for our next trip into town, we must have money, but all we could get from the paymasters was ten shillings (50p) per week in hospital blues. We had noticed that the city was full of American airmen from a nearby base; they always had plenty of cash, and they would be interested in a new Luger. Next afternoon, we took one of the pistols into town and asked the first Yanks we found if they wanted to buy one. As they looked at it in a shop doorway, I had to remind them that it was fully loaded with twelve rounds, and to treat it with respect. They bought it for 5,000 francs (£5.00), which was about a week's wage at that time. We shared out the money and went shopping. I bought a watch, and some beautiful ribbons for my sister's baby Marian, who was two years old.

A big club had opened for servicemen, called the Montgomery. While an orchestra played, we had egg and chips and an artist did a pencil portrait of me, in a few minutes for as many francs.

My hand was improving every day, and my Canadian friend's shoulder was almost healed. The Sergeant who had had his leg off above the knee was still in bed. We used to put him on a bedside mat and slide him up and down the corridors at great speed on the highly polished floors. One day the Sister came in and could not believe it when she saw his empty bed. She came in search of him, and as she went through the door we almost knocked her flying as we came back with the Sergeant at full speed.

She said, 'You Airborne lads are all alike: mad as hatters!'

It was time to sell my last pistol; the money had run out all too quickly, so off we went to find another customer, a Yank of course. The only one we could find that day wanted to pay much less than £5.00.

'How do I know it works?' he said.

I cocked it, took the magazine off to show him it was full, pushed it back in the butt and held it up in the air to fire.

He said, 'OK bud, I guess it's alright.'

I don't think he had ever seen a Luger before in his life, let alone a German face to face if it comes to that, but he paid up. Off we went to the Montgomery club for another meal and a bit of a farewell party. It would only be a matter of days before we were discharged, as we had been in hospital more than 30 days and were entitled to a week's leave.

The Colonel came round the ward, while we stood by our beds. This was the big day. He was pleased with the way the penicillin had cleared up the mess in my hand. Two pieces of the knife could be seen deep in the palm, but I could use it and it felt great, so he discharged me that morning. My clothes were given to me in exchange for the hospital blues, and I was also given a rail ticket to Ostend Regimental Holding Unit. We said our goodbyes, and went off to the station.

A hour after I left, Madame Des Camps arrived from Ghent, with a basket full of good things for me. It was to be a month before I found out that, so great had been the disruption of civilian travel, it had taken her 36 hours to reach Brussels. I was very sorry to hear this news when a letter finally reached me back at Bulford Camp. It said that they had all seen us fly over on the way to the Rhine on the 24th March.

Ostend, with its large hotels on the sea front, was very much like Brighton. The RHU collected people from different regiments who, for some reason or other, had left their units and were ready to rejoin a battalion, and as soon as a party from a unit was collected arrangements were made to return them. It could take weeks, hanging about, wasting time. My mind was made up not to return here after my leave. I would make my own way back to the 9th, no matter where they were.

At 8am next morning everyone paraded for a roll call and an inspection. An RSM asked what the hole was in my jacket.

'A bullet hole, Sir', I said.

'Why did you not mend it with your housewife?' (He referred to a sewing kit all soldiers carried for repairs.)

'It was destroyed, with my haversack, by a burst from an MG42.'

He was getting curious, that was obvious: he asked me to wait in his office.

After the parade, he said, 'Now tell me the whole story,' and I did. Later he took me to the stores and told the storekeeper to produce a Canadian battledress, size 13. These darker-coloured and better-made battledress were very much prized by anyone who could get hold of one. Only people well in with the Quartermaster could hope to be issued with one. He also replaced all the kit I had lost: towel, socks etc., and got me away on leave in a few hours.

All at home were really pleased to see that I was in good shape. I think my mother must have shown everyone my smock, jacket and shirt with the hole in, and the cross that saved my life. It was wonderful to be home again and to see the people I loved, and to think that I once thought, 'I may never see them again.'

The daily news contained information about the advance the 6th Airborne were making, and I followed every move on the map. I hired a car and enjoyed running around in it for a week, visiting different people out of town, though I did not go any further than Redcar, since petrol was still limited. But every time the 6th Division was mentioned I felt a fraud, and for once I was glad to be going back where I belonged.

On landing at Calais, instead of getting the train to Ostend RHU, I joined a battalion of Canadians just come over from England. They were heading for Nijmegen in Holland, which would be the start of my journey into Germany. When I explained to the Canukes, as we called them, what I was doing, they hid me under the seat until the RTO's (Regimental Transport Officers) had checked each coach and the train had set off. The Canadians were very good and shared their food and drink with me as we travelled through the night. We arrived early next morning in Nijmegen, where I visited a Military Police Office and made a note from the map on the wall, drawing a straight line between the towns I had heard the 6th Div. had taken. Their line of advance was towards the Elbe, passing through Celle.

As I left the MP office, I met a chap I had been to school with. His name was Laurence Simpson, he was in the Artillery and, amazingly, who should be standing beside his vehicle but Ron Sturdy! I gave them a chunk of cake which my mother had given me, and an account of the journey I was doing. Ron told me that he had visited Arnhem, just a few miles away, and had seen the mess. He assured me that he had made the right decision by staying in the Royal Scots. We said our goodbyes and wished each other luck, then I went on my way.

Later I heard that he had been cleaning his wagon down with petrol-soaked rags for inspection, and his overalls were pretty well soaked too, when someone had walked by and dropped a lighted cigarette end. In seconds, he was a mass of flames. He ran and jumped into a trough of water, but by this time he had terrible injuries. During the three years that followed, he spent months in hospital having skin grafts. It was in fact 1950 before I heard about his misfortune, and I could not help saying, 'If you had come with me into the Airborne, you might have been luckier!'

Just before reaching the famous Nijmegen bridge, I got my first lift, in a Staff car going to Münster. It was 6pm when we arrived and, seeing signs of the Staffordshire Regiment outside a building, I asked at the guard room for the RSM. He was intrigued with my story and sent his orderly to draw bedding, then showed me where I could sleep and took me to the cook house. The cook was ordered to give me a meal, and also provide me with a packed meal for my journey the next day. 'Marvellous service!' I thought, and it was certainly appreciated. I had no idea where the next bed or meal would come from. I had to make arrangements on the spot, wherever each evening found me.

My next point on the map was Osnabrück. An American convoy picked me up, and a big coloured chap, half eating and half smoking a big cigar, was very good company, and seemed to be enjoying his war. Three miles past Osnabrück, the American turned west and said 'Cheerio'.

The road I wanted was Hannover, and on the way to Minden a jeep pulled up and a couple of Yanks said 'Hop in!' They tore along at a hell of a rate, passing through Minden and on to an autobahn leading to Hannover. There was hardly a wall along the way that stood twelve feet. It was very windy and the dust was blowing about in dark clouds. The Americans turned off the Celle road, and soon an army wagon picked me up and took me into Celle.

Here I walked through the town before getting a lift for a few miles toward Ulesen. Somewhere here we passed Belsen Camp and I saw some of the inmates still sitting about in their striped clothing. Then I was walking again, and I saw a jeep parked just off the main road. Two lads were erecting a tent as I approached the jeep, which had a pair of legs sticking out from underneath. When I asked who was in charge, a voice from under the jeep said, 'Are you from Middlesbrough?' and came up to say Hello. He was a sergeant in the Signal Corps, laying a telephone line with his two assistants, and it turned out that he used to work for the GPO telephone service in Middlesbrough.

They had a good supply of food and one of the lads was a good cook. The Sergeant and I shared one of the tents. He pulled a bottle of Scotch out of his kitbag, saying he had been saving it for a special occasion: 'The war's just about over, so here's to us and a better future!' Close by, German fighter 'planes were coming in to land with white silk scarves tied to their aerials. The Russians were advancing at a good rate too and were already in Berlin, not very far away. Pilots were making sure they were taken prisoner by the Allies.

Early the next morning the Signal Corps gave me some sandwiches and ran me down the road to a good spot for a lift. A three-ton truck came along, following a route to a Bailey bridge which had been rebuilt a few days earlier to get the Airborne across the Elbe river. A sign said 'Berlin 100 kilometres', and as we passed over a Guard shouted 'It's about over – the 6th Div. are making for Wismar on the Baltic'. Twenty miles further on, the truck arrived at a supply depot, so I jumped out and started walking.

I walked for three miles and never saw a sign of life anywhere. The weather was lovely, the sun shining and the countryside looked so fresh and green. Apart from the steel telegraph poles, it was just like being in England. Turning round a corner, I could see a lot of smoke, as though some farmer was burning off stubble in a field. The smoke was very dense up ahead, and then it cleared as the breeze came across the fields. I got the surprise of my life.

On each side of the road, in both fields, there were thousands of German soldiers, sitting around fires and cooking in their mess tins. Rifles were stocked in piles around each group.

I could feel their eyes glaring at me from both sides as, with my haversack on my back, I looked straight ahead and stepped out smartly, swinging one arm. It took me twenty minutes to walk past them all, and not a word was spoken. They could have done me in, and no-one would have been any the wiser, or even missed me, as I was in fact absent from the RHU in Ostend. One thing for sure, I knew that I would never forget that experience, and I never have!

I had never seen so many German soldiers before; they must have been content to sit and wait to be evacuated to prisoner of war camps in the Allied sector, and, I suppose, were glad that they were not in Russian hands.

Soon the roads had every kind of transport the German army used, pushed to either side; the 6th Guards Armour must have pushed it all clear to get on to meet the Russians. Another sign said 'Berlin 60km'. Papers and documents were blowing all over the place. I saw tanks, half tanks, staff cars, self-propelled guns and motor cycles. It was now late afternoon and still there was no sign of any British vehicles. For over an hour I walked past all this German transport, which was useless, until I came across a staff car with only one wheel over the ditch, a BMW with the plug leads pulled off under the bonnet. I replaced these and pushed a stick into the petrol tank and found it had a gallon or so still in it. That should get me the 20 kilometres to Wismar.

Then up came a jeep with three red berets in it. They were from Divisional Headquarters, and wondered where I had come from. One of them knew that the 9th had moved into Wismar on the south side, and they drove me right into Battalion HQ.

The first chap I met was Gordon Newton from 'A' Company. He gave me a cross-bar lift on a cycle to 'C' Company, who were occupying two large detached houses. He said the war was officially over, and the Russians were just half a mile down the road. The Battalion had beaten them into the town by twenty minutes, so they were in a field just outside. Gordon joined the Metropolitan Police just after the war, and became Commandant of the Hendon Police Driving School.

Reporting to the Company Commander, I told him that I should have gone to the RHU in Ostend three days ago, but had made my own way back to the Battalion. I knew he was pleased, because all he said was that he would be over to 14 Platoon in an hour, and if I was still sober he would put me under close arrest.

Chapter 13

Celebrations

The house used by my Platoon was beautiful, and had belonged to an officer in the Gestapo. As I walked in, I saw lads coming up from the cellar with their arms full of bottles. On an elegant polished table stood a baby's bath. The necks were knocked off the bottles and the contents poured into the bath, making a giant cocktail. Everyone had a glass in his hand, and one was thrust into mine as I went round shaking hands with each of them.

Corporal Cooper said to me, 'Before we do anything else, come and see where you and I are sleeping.' It was a ground-floor bedroom, with beautiful furniture; the dressing-table was covered with perfume sprays and all the bedding was silk. I jumped on the bed and sank into a lovely feathered duvet.

We went back in the dining room, with its glass chandelier over three yards in circumference, its grand piano, and its glass case with glass sliding doors fixed along one wall, full of beautiful cut-glass objects. Pots a yard high held fine indoor plants, growing up to the ceiling. Prisoners of war who had been released from a camp close by called in for a drink, and RAF and Yankee air crews all joined in the celebrations, though the war had not been officially declared over: it was only the 3rd May.

It was wonderful being back among my friends again, all of us exchanging stories of our experiences since last we met, though a few more had been killed and others wounded. The Yanks had been on the 6th Airborne Division's right flank, and both had made rapid strides into the heart of Germany after the crossing of the Rhine. At Greven the Yanks called a halt. The opposition was too heavy, and called for an air strike before they tried again. The 9th Battalion were told to take a footbridge over the river Ems, leading into the town of Greven. 14 Platoon were leading, and Lieutenant Mc Guffie had charged across the bridge in a hail of machine-gun fire, and was killed. The remainder of the Platoon got across the bridge, holding the ground while 'C' Company joined them. The rest of the Battalion forced their way into the town under fierce fire, killed most of the enemy and took a few prisoners. The Yanks could not believe it had been done in less than two hours. They cancelled the air strike and did their best to keep up with 6th Airborne, who left them behind.

It had not been too bad for those speeding through Germany on the backs of the Guards' armoured tanks, which had blasted any opposition before the boys tore in to finish it off.

The singing was now in full swing, just like at New Year in Scotland. My head was beginning to feel split in two, so I made my way to bed, just collapsing on to it. During the night I wanted to be sick, and had to put my head out of the window. It was next morning that I found that the window had been closed at the time, but not one cut had I sustained. There was only one piece of glass still lodged in my collar.

The mess in the dining room was absolutely unbelievable. Ex-prisoners of war were laid out under the table and across chairs and the lovely chandelier was on the floor (someone had tried swinging on it across the room). Very few people could face breakfast, but I had not eaten since yesterday morning, so I made sure of mine. I heard that the CO, Napier Crookenden, had been to dinner with the Russians the night before, and was carried back on a stretcher. It seems that they had toasted everyone they could think of with vodka.

Just down the road, a harbour the size of Whitby was full of sailing craft, from fishing boats to yachts and from motor boats to canoes. There was a much bigger boat sticking out of the water, probably sunk by bombing. The glorious weather was continuing and a few of the lads were bathing in the warm sunshine. I dived in and swam over to the superstructure of the sunken boat, but soon came back when I saw all the oil floating nearby.

The harbour was coming alive, as the boys took what they liked. A yacht was under full sail, and three canoes and a dinghy were messing about. Two lads with a motor boat must have been having trouble with its engine: they had the cover off the engine compartment. Three German girls took off all their clothes and started swimming; they knew we were not allowed to speak to them, and made the most of it in the way of displaying themselves. We too were 'skinny dipping' as the Yanks called it.

Suddenly the motor boat engine came to life, rewarding the efforts of the two happy lads. They got up speed, making sharp turns and rendering it difficult for the canoes to keep afloat. Then finally they cut one of the canoes in half, causing great delight to those watching. It seemed that everyone was having fun not showing the slightest respect for anything German. They had seen the sickening sights of Belsen concentration camp and all the other terrible things during the last year. A very bitter feeling existed among the front line troops towards anything German: they had seen at first hand just what the Boche were capable of doing.

Back at our house, there were two lads who fancied themselves as pianists, and others with almighty hangovers who did not appreciate their efforts. When they came back from their meal, the pianists found the lid nailed down and, in their attempt to take the nails out, the lid came off; the music lessons continued however. The next time, they came back to find all the keys had been painted with thick white paint from the garage; they removed this with ease, using curtains pulled from the windows. But the final stage put an end to all practice with wire-cutters. Each string had been carefully cut at both ends.

The sentry called me out to see to a woman who was at the gate. She said she was worried about her plants, they would need water. I told the wife of the Gestapo house owner that they had been 'watered' every day. I am afraid that the discovery in the house of an instrument resembling a cat-o'-nine-tails had not increased our respect for its owners.

The prisoners of war were on their way down to transport arranged for them. It would take them on their first stage home. It was back to soldiering again: the Company Commander was sober, and he had seen the state of the house. He would inspect it again in two hours.

Six lads started digging a hole, 2 x 3 yards and a yard deep, in the garden at the back of the house, while everyone else collected anything loose and placed it on the large blue carpet in the centre of the room. The wall cupboards were swept clean and all the glass, broken or not, went on to the carpet. So did six wireless sets, all DC. It was alternating current in the house, and a pile of burned-out sets had accumulated before an AC set was found or taken from another house. When the hole was finished, we all took hold of the carpet edges and carried it out to the hole and dropped it in. When it was covered and raked smooth, even the garden looked smart.

Meanwhile the floors had been mopped clean and spotless. Major Dyer was amazed when he walked round, and finally he said, 'I don't know how you did it, but it's very good.'

The owner of one of the boats was ordered to take a few of us out into the Baltic to an island. We spent the afternoon swimming and diving off the boat.

A young woman was noticed passing up and down in front of the house. She would stop to adjust her shoe, letting her dress blow over her head. She did not have any pants on. Later on, I saw her coming back from the rear of the house holding bars of chocolate. I suspected our two pianists had found another source of amusement.

It was the 7th May and we were leaving. We marched to an airfield five miles away, where there were several jet fighter 'planes parked on the runway, like the ones I saw coming over the Rhine. All the German troops must have fled back towards the Elbe, in case the Russians got hold of them. We all fixed ourselves up with the flying boots the Luftwaffe used, also sheepskin coats from the stores, all brand new, and we bivouacked around the field. Next morning, Dakotas landed to take us back home. The flight took us three hours, and we arrived back in Bulford Barracks in time for the mid-day meal. I had been made Sergeant, and was able to enjoy all the comforts and privileges of the Sergeants' Mess, and also a room to myself in the barracks.

The war in Europe was finally over. We had been through a lot, and lost some very good friends, but I would not have missed the experience or the honour of working with such men in the finest battalion in the British Army. Our experiences had bound us together in friendship for life, in a way not always understood by civilians. The 6th Airborne Division had suffered 1,500 casualties, killed and wounded, on the Rhine crossing alone, plus those who lost their lives on the advance into Germany to meet the Russians.

On our return home from leave in July, we found the Battalion was back up to full strength with newly trained Para. It was also nice to see a few back from hospitals, recovered from wounds received in Normandy and Germany. My new Platoon was mainly recruits who had just completed Para training, and who were mostly older than me. I found there was an undercurrent of resentment at having a nineteen-year old Sergeant. It came to a head during an exercise we did, and I was placed on my first charge, on form 252, for their inefficiency during the scheme.

We returned to the barracks very tired, and while the rest of the Battalion went off to shower and have a meal, my Platoon marched down to the gym, much to their surprise. Here I told them what a bloody shower they were, and invited them one at a time to join me in the boxing ring, to clear the air. I was in fact terrified, because at least eight of them were as big and heavy as myself, and it was a great relief that no-one wanted to step forward. Two corporals and I drilled them on the square for over half an hour before they were dismissed.

The tonic worked well, there were no more incidents and the Platoon got over its problem. I was told off by our new Company Commander, Hugh Pond, for allowing the lads to cause trouble in the first place, but I got away with a reprimand.

An advance party was sent to India; the Japs were still fighting, and our next move would be to Burma. All kit had been exchanged for jungle green, and special brown boots were issued. A new rifle was introduced, with a short barrel and flash eliminator, supposed to be useful in jungle warfare.

Sergeant Creasey had returned from leave with the news that he had broken off his engagement, and had a ring for sale. The ring had cost quite a bit, but he only wanted £8 for it. It was not only that it was a bargain, but it was impossible to buy a ring in the shops. The ring was more than a week's wage, but he said he would wait for the cash.

The following week, I applied for a 48-hour pass. I could hardly wait to give Dorothy the ring. She did not know I was coming home to get engaged.

On Friday we fitted 'chutes at Netheravon airfield and waited for the wind to drop. I had my pass in my pocket, and would make a dash for the station as soon as the drop was completed. Soon the wind had calmed down; at 3pm the Dakotas took off and we jumped. Landing, we rolled our 'chutes, then I was off to catch the train to Waterloo. I missed the connection at King's Cross, so travelled through the night, getting home early the next morning.

My mother was away at Scarborough, so I went to Dorothy's home and had breakfast with her. That very morning, the news on the radio was the best I ever heard. The Japanese had surrendered and all members of HM forces could take an extra 48 hours' leave. We were so happy to be together at this time: it was wonderful news.

That night we went to the Coatham Hotel dance at Redcar with all our friends, including Bill Monahan. During the evening I took Dorothy out on to the hotel balcony, and slipped the ring on her finger. It had never occurred to me till then that it might not fit! But it fitted her perfectly, and Dorothy was amazed to think that I had kept it a secret all day.

I cannot remember a happier time than that day: the war was over, the lights were on again, and we had our future together to look forward to; and best of all, I would not be going to fight the Japs. Our friends were delighted to hear of our engagement, and showered us with congratulations, and Bill Monahan asked the the band to play our favourite tune, 'Long Ago and Far Away'. It just put the cream on our wonderful event.

People danced in the street that night in Redcar; some of the boys went down to the sea for a paddle, and everyone was high as a kite. On the way home along the trunk road, we found a fairground still in operation, even though it was 2am. Jimmie Burns was first out of the packed car, then we all joined him on the 'Chair-O-Planes'. It seemed no-one was going to bed: excitement and revelry was going on all over the country.

It was 6am when Dorothy reached her home to find Harry feeding the chickens in the back garden. The Ministry of Food encouraged people to 'Dig for victory', and to keep pigs and hens. Harry was, of course, delighted to hear of our engagement, and told Dorothy to run upstairs and show her Mum the ring, while he came in with a bowl of new-laid eggs and cooked us a wonderful breakfast. May then joined us with her own congratulations and said how pleased she was for us.

That night we went to the Constantine College dance with all our friends. May told us to bring a few of them back for supper, and it came as a great surprise to find that she had made us a big engagement cake and had it beautifully iced with our names on it. She had prepared a grand party, and the people in her confidence had brought us presents.

The next day my parents arrived home from their holidays. They had received a letter from my sister with the news of our engagement. I fully expected to see them as pleased as May and Harry, but it was just the reverse. My mother said she was not at all pleased, and was very disappointed in me. Poor Dad said nothing: he would not have dared!

When leave ended and I arrived back at Camp, I was met by Tom Stroud, now back with us after his wounds had healed. This man had silenced three machine-gun nests at the Merville Battery on D-Day, and his only reward had been promotion to Corporal. So much for the distribution of medals and awards!

In some cases they were a bit of a farce. It seems to me that all CO's received the DSO, and Company Commanders the MC. They had had the responsibility for conducting the jobs and seeing that they were completed; however, there were many other exploits that should have been recognised.

For example, Jock Lepper, my Platoon Commander, with Gus Gower, had gone deep into enemy territory in Normandy for several miles through deep floods, to report on the damage done to bridges over the river Dives, under the very noses of the German defenders. They were only able to move about at night, and were away for three days. The only part of it that Jock would relate to us was that, when running away from a German patrol, his trouser buttons came off: the strain of his heavy wet clothes had been too much for the cotton. He had to hold his trousers up with one hand.

Once again we paraded in the dining hall to hear about our next move, to a place called Palestine: 'A beautiful country, warm sunshine, orange trees, and Jews who are fighting with their neighbours, the Arabs. We have to go and stand between them. Leave is being arranged, after which we will sail from Southampton at the end of August.'

The Palestine posting is a story on its own. Suffice it to say, that I was there for a year, and during that time Dorothy wrote almost every day and I did the same. I was promoted to Quartermaster at the 6th Division training school, and had a very good future ahead of me if I had signed on as a regular soldier but, relinquishing the rank of Colour Sergeant, I returned home to prepare for demobilisation.

Just after my 21st birthday, Dorothy and I were married, on Boxing Day 1946. My special Canadian battle dress came out of the wardrobe for this occasion at St Stephen's Church, Woodlands Road. May and Harry made all the arrangements, and could not have been kinder. Dorothy and I left everyone having a great time at the reception and caught the train for Newcastle. In our large suitcase I carried only my toothbrush and shaving gear, and Dorothy had only some light clothing and a nightdress. Civilians had to give coupons for clothing, and few had more than one set of any item, other than underwear. The best hotel on Tyneside then was the Grand Hotel in the Haymarket. The young pageboy reached for our case to show us to our room, but I grabbed hold of it, assuring him that it was too heavy for him. Our dinner that night cost five shillings for the four courses, and the bill for the three days we were there only came to £3.

We did not know then that we had begun a partnership of long and lasting love and understanding, during our many struggles to establish a home and family.

Our six grandchildren may find the story amusing and interesting, if not now, then in years to come. Dorothy enjoyed typing and re-living these experiences once again, and I am very grateful for her patience and assistance, as always.